Glenn & Sue Hawks
119 Don Felipe Way
Ojai, Calif 93023

The Way Back to

HEAVEN

ALSO BY S. MICHAEL WILCOX

———————

BOOKS

Don't Leap with the Sheep: And Other Scriptural Strategies for Avoiding Satan's Snares

Face to Face: Seeking a Personal Relationship with God

Finding Hope: Where to Look for God's Help

Fire in the Bones: William Tyndale, Martyr, Father of the English Bible

House of Glory: Finding Personal Meaning in the Temple

Land of Promise: Images of Book of Mormon Lands

Sunset: On the Passing of Those We Love

The Ten-Day Daughter

10 Great Souls I Want to Meet in Heaven

Walking on Water and Other Classic Messages

What the Scriptures Teach Us about Adversity

What the Scriptures Teach Us about Prosperity

What the Scriptures Teach Us about Raising a Child

When Your Prayers Seem Unanswered

Who Shall Be Able to Stand? Finding Personal Meaning in the Book of Revelation

TALKS ON CD

The Fourth Watch: Receiving Divine Help When Your Prayers Seem Unanswered

House of Glory: Finding Personal Meaning in the Temple

How Will I Know? Making the Marriage Decision

The Jesus We Need to Know

King Noah Blindness and the Vision of Seers

The Michael Wilcox Collection

Of Lions, Dragons, and Turkish Delight: C. S. Lewis for Latter-day Saints

Seeing as God Sees: Discovering the Wonder of Ourselves and Others

Walking on Water: When the Lord Asks the Impossible

When All Eternity Shook

The Way Back to
HEAVEN

THE PARABLE OF THE
CRYSTAL STAIRS

S. MICHAEL WILCOX

DESERET
BOOK

Salt Lake City, Utah

To the woman who waits at the top of the stairs

Library of Congress Cataloging-in-Publication Data

Wilcox, S. Michael, author.

    The way back to heaven : the parable of the crystal stairs / S. Michael Wilcox.

        pages cm

    Includes bibliographical references and index.

    ISBN 978-1-60907-905-5 (hardbound : alk. paper)

1. Salvation—Mormon Church. 2. The Church of Jesus Christ of Latter-day Saints—Doctrines. 3. Mormon Church—Doctrines. I. Title.

    BX8643.S25W55 2015

    234—dc23   2014045036

Printed in the United States of America

Publishers Printing, Salt Lake City, UT

10 9 8 7 6 5 4 3 2 1

CONTENTS

INTRODUCTION: THE POWER OF PARABLE ix

PROLOGUE: THE CRYSTAL STAIRS 1

1. THE WASTELAND AND THE WANDERERS 7

2. THE STAIRWAYS OF MEN 21

3. THE CRYSTAL STAIRS AND THE STAIR BUILDER 34

4. SHATTERING THE STAIRS 44

5. CLIMBING THE CRYSTAL STAIRS 59

6. THE ASCENT CONTINUES 95

7. THE CITY AT THE TOP OF THE STAIRS 117

EPILOGUE: "PASS AND CONTINUE BEYOND" 135

NOTES 137

INDEX 141

Whoso cometh in at the gate
And climbeth up by me
Shall never fall

—MOSES 7:53

And he dreamed, and behold
A ladder set up on the earth,
And the top of it reached to heaven

—GENESIS 28:12

THE POWER OF PARABLE

I have multiplied visions,
And used similitudes.

—HOSEA 12:10

S ometime in my early life—in the dawning of my awareness
that God had truths to share with me, and goodness to instill
within me, and beauty to show me if I would listen, and be open,
and observe—I received, in a few brief moments of internal seeing, a key to life. It came in a series of images somewhat like a
parable—"The Parable of the Crystal Stairs"—and I have learned
from it ever since. God is a gracious and a giving God. As my life
progressed, I came to view with greater clarity and appreciation
the interior landscape that played out in the creative drama of my

mind, and was able to more thoughtfully apply its realities to the lives and experiences around me.

Perceptions given or enhanced by the Spirit are living things and grow continually throughout our lives. Their ability to guide and grant truth never diminishes. This is especially true of the scriptures and of the temple, and particularly true of the figurative, the symbol, the story, the similitude, the parable. That is the way of God. That is part of what it means to be infinite. God always runs ahead of our needs and, in his anticipatory seeing, prepares the way. Our job is to pay attention, to remember, and then to draw strength, insight, and intelligence from life's encounters, God's gifts, and past endowments of mercy. We then come to understanding, recognition, and, above all, wakefulness. In that wakefulness we learn to be compassionate, to be kind, to show mercy, to love, and to be non-judging—to want as our deepest desire to think and feel and see just as Christ and the Father do.

The Parable of the Crystal Stairs has one dominant, clarifying vision—*there is only one way to get to heaven.* This sounds obvious, but it is remarkable how many people have uncertainty about it, either in an unexamined, overconfident feeling that their way is *the* way, to the exclusion of all others, or in believing it doesn't much matter, as all roads lead to Rome, or they are simply apathetic or agnostic. To find that singular way back to heaven is humanity's highest searching. I am a Latter-day Saint speaking to Latter-day Saints, and though we may feel quite comfortable on our path—and with our plan—if we're not careful we'll miss the whole point and get lost in the details of living a Mormon life. I fear too many of us live in a lingering sense of inadequacy and misty guilt, weights from which we would be liberated. Jesus came to show us not only how to climb but also how to remove the burdens we will allow Him to remove so that the stairs rising before us may not seem so insurmountable.

Ultimately I have come to believe that the climb—the ascent up the crystal stairs—has more to do with *being* and *becoming* than believing and doing. For me, that is the essential, never-to-be-forgotten truth. They are deeply interwoven but do not balance equally across the beam when weighed. Being and becoming almost always lead to correct and proper believing and doing, but the reversal of those positions does not necessarily hold true. We will explore this. People are usually somewhat surprised to learn that faith, in its earliest definition, seemed not so much centered on our assenting to a set of statements about God's nature and our relation to Him as much as it was focused on creating our character—the way we see and treat others, our pattern of thinking, and the quality of our soul. The stairs are there to help us on our upward journey; we all have different steps on which to work. All are beautiful when mastered. Those that are easy for you may be a lifelong struggle for me. In a sense, the placement and sequence of the stairs are individualized for us in our Father's grand mercy and wisdom. We also all carry with us various bundles and packages which we must part with if our climb is to be successful. Those can be painful and soul-stretching moments. I have stared into the contents of my own burdens with both a desire for release and a tenacious grip that whispers, "In time, yes, but not now." Yet the stairs forever beckon and we would be home.

Joseph Smith once wrote to William W. Phelps—perhaps the most poetic soul of the Restoration—"Oh, Lord, when will the time come when Brother William, Thy servant, and myself, shall behold the day that we may stand together and gaze upon eternal wisdom engraven upon the heavens, while the majesty of our God holdeth up the dark curtain until we may read the round of eternity, to the fulness and satisfaction of our immortal souls? Oh, Lord, deliver us in due time from the little, narrow prison, almost as it were, total darkness of paper, pen and ink;—and a crooked, broken, scattered and imperfect language."[1] I believe parables and stories—the figurative, images, metaphors, and symbols—are one of the ways the Lord holds up that dark curtain. We see rather than read; we sense rather than reason. So I offer a parable here in the hope that it may enable us to see, perhaps just a tiny bit more clearly, "the round of eternity" and our place within it.

I do not remember the context in which this parable came to me; it happened so very long ago. I have no recollection of the catalyst, the source of contemplation that marked its creation. Perhaps that is best. Only the images have remained, but they have nourished me for a lifetime. I will portray the Parable of the Crystal Stairs in the pages that follow as I recall that first experience and subsequent pondering, followed by what I have learned from life and from the scriptures about the setting of the stairs, the distracting stairways of the world, the burdensome packages we all carry that delay our desired ascent, and, most importantly, a discussion about the Stair Builder and the beauty of some of the individual stairs we must climb. What awaits at the top of the stairs came to my understanding later in life and continues to be refined. I conclude with those insights.

THE CRYSTAL STAIRS

And thine ears shall hear
A word behind thee, saying,
This is the way, walk ye in it.

—Isaiah 30:21

We are walking on a vast, empty plain stretching to the farthest limits of vision, crisscrossed with pathways that reach in all directions. The sky overhead is blanketed in mist and cloud, fog hanging low to the ground in patches obscuring our view. The sunshine is muted, coming from an indistinct direction. In the distance, buildings of some sort loom out of the fog, their shape or purpose not yet determined. We are travelers; there are thousands like us scattered over the wasted land, which is hard surfaced and rock strewn. Little growth breaks the stretching vista. And it is dark, a land where life struggles to breathe, to grow, to reach skyward, to see. All of the numberless paths lead somewhere, but none seem inviting or promising. We are a little frightened, like lost children.

We and the rest of the wanderers spread over the plain, searching. Somehow we know this is not home—that home is somewhere above and beyond the clouds and darkness. We all know this instinctively and will gaze heavenward as if looking for a way out. We are driven by a hunger for climbing, for reaching. *Up* draws us more than *out*, or *away*. But how do we move up? We are homesick, but have no recollection of any other place we might have lived. It seems as if we have always been on the wasteland, have never known any other life but that of a wanderer. We look at those around us. They are travelers too, for each is carrying something—packages, boxes, suitcases, bundles, backpacks of various shapes and sizes. We look down the various roads and off into the distance, seeking direction yet always glancing upwards. Every soul is filled with longing.

Most of us travel alone or in small groups, but ultimately everyone is drawn to the structures towering in the distance. They appear to be some kind of building; we travel quickly in their direction. Movement of any kind is relieving. In the parting mists as we draw nearer we can see a large, unfinished stairway reaching heavenward, feverish activity surrounding it. Its builders are intent and earnest. The stairway is made of stone; its creators persuasively discuss its strengths with the wanderers who approach. Down another path, a different stairway is being erected, this one of brick. Dozens of stairways climb toward the sky, some circling, some steep, some solid, others supported by pillars—none finished.

We find staircases of wood, of metal, of earth, and every combination of mortar, stones, and steel as we wander from one to another where they are scattered across the plain. A close look reveals that not all activity is devoted to lifting the stairs higher. Much time is spent on repairs, additions, replacements, new ideas and altered blueprints that change the rise and pitch of the respective staircases.

But in spite of stylistic twists and fortifying buttresses, they share one common feature. Their foundations all rest on earth. They build from the ground up. Ultimately the weight of adding stair upon stair upon stair becomes too great and the staircases begin to tumble upon themselves. Some are abandoned, others are surrounded by multitudes who scurry to repair what has fallen. Mixed within the confidence and assurances of the builders is a sense of hidden anxiety or of growing frustrated indifference.

In the center of the wasteland, the clouds draw aside, a light radiating toward the ground. Within the light a stairway lowers, but it is different than all the others scattered across the landscape. It is created entirely of crystal. Each stair is delicate, refined, and appears so fragile a touch would break its beauty. Balanced lightly a few inches above the earth, the stairs seem to breathe with their own life. Each is etched with beautiful designs, all unique, none duplicating another. Each stair of crystal, rising in a gentle ascent only a few inches above the step beneath, forms a prism through which light shines. Thus every engraved stair splits the brightness flowing through it into all the colors of the rainbow, and this paints the clouds in glory and warms the earth with reds, yellows, oranges, greens, and blues. I cannot describe the effect it had on me. I could not take my eyes off it; this same pull affected others, for soon people came from all directions and gathered in the spectrum of colored light at the foot of the stair. The stillness of the scene was finally broken by a questioning voice, "Beautiful, yes. But can it be climbed?"

That last question, asked not with cynicism but real worry, breaks the spell of the staircase's beauty somewhat, and we look at those thin wedges of glass for the first time with experienced eyes. Will they hold us? We wonder not only about the entire flight of stairs, but about each individual one. Would a single weak step among the many that ascend be perilous, given their delicate nature? As if to stop our thoughts from growing into doubts that would prevent our climb, a being appears, standing on the first stair just a few inches off the earth. He appears to be as old as the ages yet as young as a newborn child. All the innocence of creation's dawn and all the wisdom of everlasting worlds are visible in Him and we know at once He is the Stair Builder. He speaks only a few words, pleasantly and unhurried, in mildness and invitation. "My stairs are strong! You may climb them; I will show you the way." He smiles, turns, and one by one begins to climb the prisms that rise into the clouds.

The impact of the Stair Builder's words is felt immediately. Belief and hope rise in the eyes of those gathered in the rainbow light. Though a few—unbelieving still—walk in the direction of the stairs of wood and stone, most are ready to climb. They shoulder their loads and approach the stairs. But a strange and unsettling thing happens as the first climber places his foot on the thin glass. It shatters—and the surprise could not have been more unexpected. But more than the shattering of the step, what happens to the bits of broken glass fill us with amazement. Rather than falling to the ground only inches away, they dissipate in the air for the briefest of moments before re-forming the stair as though no weight had ever been placed upon it. Once again it floats just above the ground, inviting the traveler to climb. The climber makes a second attempt and again the step shatters and reforms. Others try with the same lack of success.

For a few moments we are confused, but then notice that we all have one thing in common. We carry suitcases, bags, and bundles—some large, some small, each different from the others, each peculiar to its owner. The travelers, noting the weights they carry, begin to divide into groups. Some converse for a while, then open their backpacks and suitcases. They inventory their possessions and then close their bags with regret. Perhaps the crystal stairs are not what has been promised. Many of these wanderers shoulder their bags, turn, and walk away to attempt the stairways of men. Brick, stone, or steel, they reason, will hold weight the crystal stairs will not allow.

Others watch them go, then turn to the spectrum of light and sort through their belongings, laying some aside. The stairs are so beautiful and rise so high—into the clouds and out of sight. Carrying a lighter load, they face the stairs and take that first step. But the stairs shatter and re-form just as before. Once more the travelers lay down their bundles and sort through their remaining possessions, but there is always something with which they cannot part, something they prefer to keep instead of climbing, and in time they also turn away to try the manmade stairs. Will they not find escape from the wasteland and happiness there?

The remaining travelers watch the others go, then, summoning their courage and without looking too deeply into their own packages, put them aside, and approach the waiting stairs. Each traveler steps hesitantly onto the bottom stair, but this time it holds. With renewing confidence they step forward and up once again, and once again the stair is solid. Step by step they climb, and step by step the view becomes more glorious, the light more intense. But, to our surprise, some stop and stare in disbelief at the next higher stair, looking intently at the etchings. Each traveler stops at a seemingly random height. Though all the stairs have held firm, for some unexplained reason they fear the next one up. Will it hold them too? Some try to bypass the particular stair that seems to trouble them, but their attempt is thwarted by the familiar shattering, dissipating, and re-forming of that stair. The stairs allow only one step at a time; none can be bypassed.

Some travelers stand paralyzed, immobile, neither retreating nor moving forward. Some descend, retracing their steps, but then move toward the stairways waiting in the distance. Most, however, keep their eyes on the Being that climbs the stairs ahead of them, never looking down, trusting each step as they approach it, and, in time, climb out of our view and into the increasing light above the clouds. We, too, would be off the wasteland. Higher happiness awaits us, so we approach the stairs.

As we climb, the plain below recedes farther and farther into the distance. Soon even the other rising stairways are only tiny dots scattered over the stretching land. We notice that the light increases as we pass each step and that the Stair Builder always climbs slowly before us. We also discern that as we progress the climb seems to become easier, as if the pull of the earth is lessening. Each stair is conquered more quickly now. In time, the wasteland disappears completely and the light is so intense we can almost feel it passing through us, so that if we looked behind we might see no shadows. We pass the clouds and still the light increases. It is warm, but the warmth is more than physical. There is love and joy and peace within it. Eventually we stand on the final stair and see in the distance a beautiful city, also made of crystal. Its gate is open, there are no doors, and we are surprised to see how broad the central street is. Have we not heard of the narrowness of the way? The buildings are all different and, as with the stairs, when the light shines through their many angles and edges it is split into a spectrum of color of which the rainbow is but a foreshadowing. The Stair Builder is waiting in the entrance. He smiles at us and says a single word: "Look!"

CHAPTER ONE

THE WASTELAND AND THE WANDERERS

O Lord, wilt thou not shut the gates
Of thy righteousness before me,
That I may walk in the path
Of the low valley.

—2 NEPHI 4:32

THE LONE AND DREARY WORLD

I have often pondered the opening scene of the crystal stairs with some amazement, for I knew even in my younger years that the wasted plain represented our mortal existence, and yet I was born loving life and the world with all its wonders. This is a splendid place! What a lovely classroom God created for us to be schooled within. There is so much light, so much beauty and goodness, so very many things to wonder at and love. Did not God pronounce at the end of each creative day that everything was good, including man and woman—all was "very good"? (Genesis 1:31). I think of trips to Yosemite, the northern California redwoods, the red and orange glow of Bryce Canyon and Zion National Parks, vivid sunsets on the California coast with the sound of the surf, the faces of children, the refined beauty of women—so much creative graciousness present in our day-to-day existence; how could my life here be depicted as a granite-crusted earth deficient of green, barren of the lovely music of nature, fog shrouded in twilight gray?

Yet Lehi wrote, "Methought I saw in my dream, a dark and dreary wilderness," later continuing with, "I beheld myself that I was in a dark and dreary waste," and "after I traveled for the space of many hours in darkness" (1 Nephi 8:4–8). Outside of the Garden of Eden, our first parents found themselves also in the lone and dreary world. The words can seem so alien to all we know of life on this beautiful planet—"dark," "dreary," "waste," "lone." Are there sadder words written? I do not perceive life that way. The repetitive truth of these images is verified in the Lord's House, but with greater insight. In that lone, dreary, and wasted world, the prince of darkness reigns. He would be there, too, demanding his tribute of human worship, ever watchful for the pinprick crack of frailty to penetrate, deceive, and mock. "Be sober, be vigilant," Peter warned, "because your adversary the devil, as a roaring lion, walketh about, seeking whom he may devour" (1 Peter 5:8).

I grew up in the 1960s in southern California. It was a decade where forests of our ethically principled foundations were questioned, then cut down, the moral landscape denuded in ways from which we have never recovered. New winds blew, strong winds, and generational erosion set in as exceptions became the rule while the topsoil of a principle-driven life was slowly washed downstream. All was change; all was challenged with very little set in its place. No, God has not made the world a wasteland— and it continually tries to regenerate the new green of divine goodness—but there are those who persist in the destruction of moral life. Teenage life in the sixties, as now, was driven by music, with much of it echoing a siren song that's difficult to turn from. I lost many friends to the spirit of the sixties. It was a watershed decade, perhaps the most critical of the twentieth century, but there the meaning of the wasteland became clear.

As a new teacher of high school students in the 1970s, I saw the same forces at work, with the same losses. It was not Lehi's spacious building with its pointing fingers that seemed to draw away so many I cherished, but the general air and atmosphere of a world where the green-giving life breath of eternal law was decaying. In an earlier century, the poet Matthew Arnold gave voice to what we see too often in the world around us:

> *The sea of faith*
> *Was once, too, at the full, and round earth's shore*
> *Lay like the folds of a bright girdle furl'd;*
> *But now I only hear*
> *Its melancholy, long, withdrawing roar,*
> *Retreating, to the breath*
> *Of the night-wind.*[1]

They are haunting words. We live in such a lovely world, filled with comfort and with hope handed down from those faith-filled grand personalities of the past. T. S. Eliot spoke of "The awful daring of a moment's surrender / Which an age of prudence can never retract / By this, and this only, we have existed."[2] That hope, the desire for that surrender is felt by us all on the wasted land as we search. We want the daring surrender, but to what?—or to whom? Perhaps the great question is what do we surrender—or how? Our ability to climb the crystal stairs will depend on the answers. We dare not make the wrong surrenders. I have talked with so many people giving in to the wasteland, even those who have seen and felt the energy and joy of the etched, radiant panels of crystal.

It was the loss of the old fathers' fervent faith I saw in the changing world of the sixties. Too many surrendered the wrong things, and that is true both individually and as a society. As a youth and as a young teacher of seminary students whom I dearly loved, I saw many making choices which led to undesirable consequences, even tragic ones. In my search for solutions, I had a dream about those straying students. The cloud-covered wasteland's meaning became painfully apparent, but with that came direction. Counsel is what we need on the wasteland. We need the messages God always promises to send and that arrive if we are alert to their coming. Wherever there is a problem projected, God will speak to it. There will be counsel! As a father, I was also deeply grateful for the new images placed in my mind.

"WE ARE WORSHIPPING"

There is a beautiful, pristine lake in the backcountry of Glacier National Park named Elizabeth. It is roughly ten miles into the wilderness; I have hiked the trail into it a dozen times. The lake's stillness mirrors the peaks above, waterfalls flowing down the mountainside and forests lining the edges like a lady dressed in her finery. She is the princess of the park in my mind and I love her. In my dream I was hiking towards the lake, anticipating the quiet and calm solitude it offered, but as I approached I could hear music—hard music—and many harsh voices. I broke through the forest that surrounds the lake a good thousand yards too soon. Someone had cut down every tree surrounding the shore—their gnawed stumps pitiful reminders of a former splendor. There were thousands of young people at the lakeside. The atmosphere was dark, the activities questionable at best, damaging and dangerous for the most part. None of them spoke to the deeper sense of who we were. It was a Montana Woodstock. The lake was polluted, mud underfoot, cans and garbage floating and drifting in piles next to the shore. All the water flowing from the glaciers could not cleanse the scenery I so loved. Concrete slabs had been poured and tin huts topped them. All was chaos, but my distress was doubled to see my students among the partying throngs. Most were not participating, but hanging at the edges—hesitant, watching, waiting, wondering: drawn, but repelled. I knew the feeling well—the loved and hated temptation, the relief of giving in and the repelling fear, the easing of desire, and the coming guilt. I knew its consequences.

I was suddenly approached by an exquisitely dressed man with immaculately combed silver-gray hair. His air was calm, knowing, controlling, watchful, and also somewhat suspicious and alert. "Welcome, Brother Wilcox," he greeted me. "We've been expecting you." I did not know who he was, but he seemed to be in charge of all the destruction so I asked him, "What have you done to my lake? And what are you doing to my students?" He considered my question, then, waving an insouciant hand over everything, casually replied, pausing between each sentence so they could have their full effect: *"Oh, this? . . . This is my church! . . . These are my members! . . . We are worshipping!"* Then I knew who he was—the Master of Waste: wasted potential, wasted goodness, wasted lives, wasted dreams, the God of the Wasteland, the voice that beckons the poor, beloved prodigals to the "far country," there to "[waste their] substance with riotous living," and end hungering with the swine (Luke 15:13).

I could see my discovery pleased him well. "Those are my students," I said with as much courage as I could summon. "You can't have them." He listened as though I were inconsequential— a slight distraction, nothing more.

"We'll see," he replied, and his tone had a touch of menace, but the voice stayed calm. "Go to them. Call them out. Be persuasive. See if what you have to offer them in your holy books can match what I give them." He seemed so sure of himself; I was frightened. But I turned to my students and tried with all the energy of soul to get them to leave the lake shore. I succeeded with only a few—those who knew I loved them.

I awoke with a desperate feeling in my heart and the image of the smiling, knowing, well-dressed man laughing at my failures. The world can be so beautiful and good—as pure as an untouched high-mountain lake. It was so created. *It is beautiful,* with all the loveliness of life mirroring godliness as the lake mirrors the mountains, but morally, we as a race, we have polluted it, age after age, society and civilization, near and far, infecting and tainting our environment with our own excuses and excesses. We are at once the creators, perpetuators, and victims of it. Is there a way out?

"COME OUT OF THE WORLD"

There are times when we dream and wake and know we never finished the story. It can be frustrating. We try to return to sleep, but it never works. We invent endings, but doubt if they are the true ones. Once, and only once, I returned to a dream and saw the end. In this case, an end that would lead me to an understanding of other aspects of the crystal stairs, and make me a better teacher, father, and friend.

I was returned in my mind to the lake—to the home ground of imagination. But this time I prayed. "What do I say, Lord? What power draws the soul from pollution?" How do we survive the lone and dreary world of muted sunshine and rock surfaces? And the answer came. "As loud as you are able, call out to them the words I will give you." Above the music and raucous laughter I called out, *"All those who love the Savior, come out of the world!"* Alma issued a similar invitation to the straying Saints in Zarahemla: "And now I say unto you, all you that are desirous to follow the voice of the good shepherd, *come ye out from the wicked, and be separate, and touch not their unclean things"* (Alma 5:57; emphasis added). It is such a simple plea—no grand, momentous words, but strength and courage arising out of love.

Like hearing a trumpet calling to battle, the students' heads snapped to attention and turned in the direction of the call. Memories of deeper love sounded as they remembered (and allowed their awareness of Him to grow) a Being whose mercy, long-suffering, and compassion they knew from a distant existence and could not entirely forget. One by one in small groups, leaning against one another, encouraging each other, calling to each other, they gathered at the head of the lake and walked down the path into the green, clear forest. They left not because they loved a teacher, a parent, a friend, or even a prophet, but because they loved their Savior. That love—discovering it, searching for it, expanding it, growing in its life breath—was the key to their journey out of the wasteland.

It is the key for us all. We will do things in our love of Christ and our Father in Heaven that we will not do for any other person or being in creation. It is the highest of motivations, beyond the need for parental, prophetic, or scriptural reminders. Those will provide clarification and experience, but love is the driving force. Jesus taught at the Last Supper, "If ye love me, keep my commandments" (John 14:15). Love comes first; obedience follows naturally. You can pound on obedience all day long and get only fearful compliance or proud self-righteousness (or defiant rebellion). If we teach the sweet truths about Jesus foremost, instead of a strong focus on the standards and commandments, those who listen will love, and, moved upon by love, leave the lake. Not only surviving the wasteland, but ascending the stairs also rests upon this.

LOVE FOR THE SHEPHERD

I have an oak tree in my backyard, a very unique oak tree. In the fall when all the other trees' leaves turn color and fall off, this tree holds on to them. They turn brown clearly enough—an ugly brown—but no wind this side of a hurricane is strong enough to separate them from their tenacious grasp. That tree used to frustrate me. I would pull at the leaves and shake the branches to no avail. The everything-must-be-in-order me was annoyed. I wanted those leaves to fall and the bare branches to look like all the other trees. If we have a heavy snowfall, I have to go outside from time to time and shake the snow off lest the branches break from the weight on their leaves. But I love that tree. It is so beautiful in green. It has taught me a great lesson. Each spring, as the new, bright-growing leaves begin to bud, they push the old, brown ones off effortlessly and grow into April splendor. I think life is similar. Sometimes we try so hard to pull off our old habits and weaknesses, but they seem so tenacious, so very reluctant to leave. But if we will replace them with good, the old falls naturally away. The greatest good is love, a love that prompts action. In Paul's hierarchy, it triumphs even over faith (see 1 Corinthians 13:13). If a choice had to be made—and fortunately it doesn't—better to love than believe; better to show compassion than to witness.

The pull of the wasteland, the celebrations at the lake—the pleasures of the world—can be very strong. They can be strong even when we don't want to indulge. Pulling alone at old habits and weaknesses is not enough. We need the power of new green leaves to release the hold of the old brown leaves. We replace old gravitational pulls with something we love more, in this case—in all cases—with the love of Christ. It isn't sufficient to urge the soul from the polluted lake or wasted plain, there must be something else to love, someone else to follow.

The Psalmist knew the soul of his shepherd God and gave us in his most touching Psalm another metaphor of the world, including the hope for traversing the wasteland. "Yea, though I walk through *the valley of the shadow of death*, I will fear no evil: for thou art with me" (Psalm 23:4; emphasis added). The visual impression of "the valley of the shadow" seems to fit so well with the images of Lehi's dark wilderness and Adam's and Eve's lone and dreary world—the wasteland. I used to think it had only to do with actual dying, but I have since learned to view it as a descriptive likeness of so much of the moral journeys of the world. However, there is the Shepherd—He who restores the soul, whose rod and staff bring comfort, the cup-runneth-over, goodness-and-mercy Shepherd. He will take us to the still waters and the green meadows. In simple words: "I shall not want" (Psalm 23:1).

We feel the Psalmist's love in that Psalm. We feel love from his Shepherd. It awakens our own love, and his prayer becomes our prayer. The more we know of Christ, the more the bonds tighten. The more clearly we see Him, the more we see the Father. And the love grows. That is why we read the scriptures—to know who He is, how He thought, what He did, how He listened, how He shared, how He forgave. The scriptures have no higher purpose. The Church has no other purpose. Somewhere among all those paths, all those shadows and dreary darkness, through the fog and mists and towering stone and brick stairways, He will be there. We need only find Him.

Paul counseled the Athenians, and through them, all of us "that they should seek the Lord, if haply they might feel after him, and find him, though he be not far from every one of us: for in him we live, and move, and have our being" (Acts 17:27–28).

"STRANGERS AND PILGRIMS"

Jacob once described this life and its people in the following manner: "Our lives passed away like as it were unto us a dream, we being a lonesome and a solemn people, wanderers" (Jacob 7:26). Paul taught a similar truth when speaking of Abraham and Sarah, who "looked for a city which hath foundations, whose builder and maker is God" (Hebrews 11:10). Their search, for what they could not realize on earth, led to their "[confession] that they were strangers and pilgrims on the earth" (Hebrews 11:13). For as long as I can remember, these verses have sounded like music in my heart, not particularly joyful, but haunting and yet not negative. I never doubted their truthfulness or that they were describing exactly what I have felt for as long as I can remember.

Early in the Restoration, the Lord touched that longing, bringing it into our own age and time and making it a positive quality. He spoke of "a city reserved until a day of righteousness shall come—a day which was sought for by all holy men . . . and confessed they were strangers and pilgrims on the earth; but obtained a promise that they should find it and see it" (D&C 45:12–13). I will never forget the ache I felt as a small boy listening in sacrament meeting to my mother singing the words, "more longing for home" contained in the hymn "More Holiness Give Me."[3] I didn't know then what I was feeling and I certainly could not have put it into words. There was just a loneliness and a yearning for I knew not what—except the inkling that I was not where I belonged eternally. As much as we love this earthly home, there is something strange and unfamiliar about it. Home, yet . . . not home, its beauty seeming more a reminder of somewhere distant—a place long forgotten yet balanced just on the brink of consciousness, our love of the creation, of beauty, arising from familiarity rather than an awareness of something new.

Paul continued his description of Abraham and Sarah, but undoubtedly unfolding the state of his own soul, finding confirmation in their experience. "They that say such things declare plainly that they seek a country. . . . But now they desire a better country, that is, an heavenly: wherefore God is not ashamed to be called their God: for he hath prepared for them a city" (Hebrews 11:14, 16). These words do magical things for us. They awake images, call things from our deepest memory. We are seeking that better country, that eternal city. We are eternal beings and this is a mortal state; it is natural to long for the everlasting. The central longing of life, for many unfulfilled, is for a compass and a motivation. Men and women have felt it long before Joseph Smith restored it to its central role in our understanding of the Father's plan of happiness.

"THOUGH INLAND FAR WE BE"

William Wordsworth, years before Joseph Smith, sensed the distant home and defended his inclinations in arguably his most famous poem (and certainly the most familiar to Latter-day Saints), titled "Ode—Intimations of Immortality from Recollections of Early Childhood." As a boy, he had felt a closeness to and hunger for the land above the mists, and though that had faded and changed with time, it remained with him and acted as the central refining agent of his life—as it can for all of us. This is not an anticipation of eternal reward for a life *well lived*, but a restoration to a life *once lived*:

Our birth is but a sleep and a forgetting:
The Soul that rises with us, our life's Star,
Hath had elsewhere its setting,
And cometh from afar:
Not in entire forgetfulness,
And not in utter nakedness,
But trailing clouds of glory do we come
From God, who is our home:
* * * * *
Hence in a season of calm weather
Though inland far we be,
Our Souls have sight of that immortal sea
Which brought us hither,
Can in a moment travel thither,
And see the Children sport upon the shore,
And hear the mighty waters rolling evermore.[4]

We can silence those intuitive instincts. We can doubt them into submission until they speak no more than the tiniest unsettling whisper, but if we heed them, they will draw us toward eternal goodness. That is their purpose.

There is a hauntingly beautiful Psalm written by an unknown captive Hebrew who had been taken to Babylon after the fall of Jerusalem. There they sat by the river and "hanged our harps upon the willows." In Babylon, "they that carried us away captive required of us a song; [they] required of us mirth, saying, Sing us one of the songs of Zion." The reply echoes the feeling of the darkened wasteland: "How shall we sing the Lord's song in a strange land?" (Psalm 137:2–4).

Much of the proving we face in life is to learn how to sing the Lord's song, even in a strange land—to find mirth and joy and gladness knowing, as the Hebrews knew, that God would bring them home again, but they must not forget. The harps would

not forever hang "by the rivers of Babylon." Their need was to remember their beloved city, which is our need also, but our homeland is an eternal one, our city "a city which hath foundations,
whose builder and maker is God" (Hebrews 11:10). The Psalm
continues in a note of triumphant remembrance: "If I forget thee,
O Jerusalem, let my right hand forget her cunning. If I do not
remember thee, let my tongue cleave to the roof of my mouth; if
I prefer not Jerusalem above my chief joy" (Psalm 137:5–6). Such
fervent remembering will carry us to the crystal stairs, where we
will learn to climb above our own rivers of Babylon. *Remember* is
such an important word. What exists above the clouds is something we are all trying to remember.

"THY SOUL'S IMMENSITY"

I believe the longing we feel as wanderers—the necessary remembering—also has to do with who we are at the very core of
our being. The Doctrine and Covenants offers a soul-expanding,
stretching vision of mankind when we read, "Ye were also in the
beginning with the Father; that which is Spirit, even the Spirit
of truth." A few verses later, this idea is repeated with greater insight. "Man was also in the beginning with God. Intelligence, or
the light of truth, was not created or made, neither indeed can
be" (D&C 93:23, 29).

To hunger for light and truth is inherent in our very nature.
Our eyes must turn inward sometimes to see, in Wordsworth's
words, "thy soul's immensity." This is the deepest, most ancient, before-time remembering. For it was not just a premortal existence Wordsworth sensed and Joseph Smith taught, but
the grandness of each individual in that former living. What
we sometimes sense as wanderers in the wasteland is the divine
within ourselves—not God's creation reaching for divinity or

eternal happiness, but the self-recognition of something older, something uncreated as section 93 revealed—a divinity inherent in who we are. In this revealed scripture, Joseph Smith lifted our understanding of God and His purposes to a higher plateau. We hunger not just for a premortal home, but for our own insoluble unity with the eternal, even with God—for we are of the same race, of the same "intelligence," or, as the Hindus say, "Thou art That."

The Apostle John elevated the early Saints' sense of themselves and showed that he knew the power of this inward-turning recognition when he wrote, "Beloved, now are we the sons of God, and it doth not yet appear what we shall be: but we know that, when he shall appear, we shall be like him; for we shall see him as he is" (1 John 3:2). There is a hint here of what waits at the top of the stairs, what we are to "look" at, but more of that later. Understanding the divinity within—which wishes to climb as an element of its very nature—led John to conclude, "And every man that hath this hope in him purifieth himself, even as he is pure" (1 John 3:3). The crystal stairs are all about that purity— the purity of being and becoming.

We wander on the wasteland seeking a way upward precisely because the wasteland is, in so many aspects, foreign and alien to what we are, to what we are destined to become. Or, if you will, alien to the fulfillment of our continued being. The central lesson of the crystal stairs is balanced on being and becoming. That is why we climb; it is the climbing itself. That is the only way to heaven. In a certain sense, heaven is you.

CHAPTER TWO

THE STAIRWAYS
OF MEN

Except the Lord build the house,
They labour in vain that build it.

—PSALM 127:1

"ONLY ONE WAY TO GET TO HEAVEN"

When I was a bishop, I used to enjoy interviewing the children very much. Their answers never ceased to amaze and surprise me. I recall interviewing a young man about ten years of age one Sunday afternoon. I would often ask the children what their favorite scripture story was. This never failed to open up opportunities for conversations. I had heard many answers to this question that gave lovely insights into the innocence of a child's mind, but I was not prepared for the answer I received. My young friend told me his favorite scripture story was the Tower of Babel. That immediately awoke my curiosity. Why would that story enchant a child? I had largely ignored that scriptural account. He related the story correctly enough so I asked him what he had learned from the building of Babel's Tower. Without hesitation, he replied, "There is only one way to get to heaven: righteousness." That was a remarkable insight! I questioned his parents, thinking they had taught him such a profound lesson, but they had not done so. It was his perception alone. It is wonderful to be taught by a child!

There are many approaches to happiness and fulfillment. Many deliver to a degree, yet not on the scale we seek. In assessing the other stairs on the wasteland, it is how high they climb and not the builders' intentions we question. The stairways of men are not inherently evil; they are not overtly false. They do rise! I have studied many of them—the philosophical, the religious, the literary, the artistic, the humanist, the stoic and the epicurean, whether millennium-old or new-age shining. To a degree, they will all lift you off the wasteland. I have found much to admire, and yes, even love. While they are not the stairs we seek, the pattern is there, the instinct to rise. When I first considered the crystal stairs, I mistrusted those other edifices of brick, stone, and wood. I read the intentions of their builders as worthy of suspicion, bordering on condemnation, but I have learned much since those first judgmental days. Now I see that their builders were constructing *stairs* on the plain, not amusement parks or strip malls. We are all trying as best we can. Any endeavor to lift, to build, to answer, even those whose efforts will never result in the tiniest peek behind the clouds, must not be viewed too severely or harshly or with a sense of superiority or even pity. Defining righteousness, which, as my young friend so valiantly stated is the only way to get back to heaven, is not always as free of ambiguity as we would wish. But we would be home. The search cannot be casual.

I have reflected over the years on Naaman's self-imposed

dilemma when told by Elisha that he must bathe seven times in the Jordan River in order to be clean of his leprosy. Enraged, he cried out in indignation, "Are not Abana and Pharpar, rivers of Damascus, better than all the waters of Israel? may I not wash in them, and be clean?" (2 Kings 5:12). So many of us have this problem. We prefer our own plans of happiness to the one designed by our Father in Heaven. We want the rivers of Damascus when it's from the Jordan that deep cleansing, healing, joy, and fulfillment comes. I don't doubt Naaman. I assume that the Abana was a good, decent river and useful for everyday cleansing. Similarly, as inviting as the many other stairways may be, as compelling as their arguments might be, we're looking for messages from our Father in Heaven, signposts to eternity, the stairs that are not only inviting to climb or beautiful to look at, but those that differ in one oh-so-critical manner—we want the stairway that comes from heaven down, not from earth up.

"NOTHING WILL BE RESTRAINED FROM THEM"

My young friend's insight caused me to reexamine the Tower of Babel story. Was I missing something that might be important and relevant? "As they journeyed from the east," we are told of those early stairway dreamers, "they found a plain. . . . And they said, Go to, let us build us a city and a tower, whose top may reach into heaven. . . . And the Lord came down to see the city and the tower, which the children of men builded. And the Lord said . . . this they begin to do: and now *nothing will be restrained from them, which they have imagined to do*" (Genesis 11:2, 4–6; emphasis added). It is an interesting story. The tower mentioned was in all probability a ziggurat—a pyramid structure with steps looking like a stairway. The very first pyramid of Egypt, that of Djoser in Saqqara, is so constructed. I used to think the Babel builders were wicked, but the story really does not give us that detail. Remember that they were the descendants of Noah's sons, and we know the names of two of them who were present at "the great tower"—Jared and his brother Moriancumer (see Ether 1:33).

Babel is confusion, and if one tower may be built, hundreds may follow. At its deepest level, the story is a comment on humankind and a tendency we have to create our own systems. This was Naaman's problem as well as those of Babel. God wants us to be creative, to solve our own problems. We are to be gods in a distant eon, and gods must reason, and create, and think, and build. God blessed us with intelligence, and we have seen in Doctrine and Covenants 93 that we have always been beings of intelligence. That intelligence is intrinsically linked to agency, and the two together equal existence itself (see D&C 93:29–30).

But what may be our greatest gift may become our greatest limitation if we believe our city is *the* city—our stair, *the* stair. We must not live independent of God and must not project ourselves onto God and think He is like us in our self-justification. Too many centuries of persecution and inhumanity have followed that reasoning. The problem in Babel (and in our world as well) was that they were building their own city, their own tower. The result would be overconfidence, living only within their own circumference, but outside the boundaries of God's city—His tower—because they could do great things themselves. According to Genesis 11, they could then do anything they imagined. There would be no restraining—the child living independent of the celestial parent, not so much out of rebelliousness, but because of the immense capacity inherent in the child's divine genes. Remember Abraham and Sarah sought "a city which [had] foundations," but ironically those foundations come from the top down, from God. The city's foundations, against all logic, are supported not from beneath, but from above—"whose builder and maker is

God" (Hebrews 11:10). Too many try to live without God, saying, "Why bother?"

THE GATE OF HEAVEN

The scriptures often offer closely placed contrasting characters, choices, or views. In literature, these are called "foils." Like the touch points of two fencing masters, the contrasting ideas or characters are set against each other. They invite comparison. Early in Genesis, the tower stairs of Babel are presented. A few chapters later, we see the opposite when Jacob, with a stone for a pillow, dreams of a stairway to heaven. But this dream comes as a gift from God—from heaven downward. "And he dreamed, and behold a ladder set up on the earth, and the top of it reached to heaven: and behold the angels of God ascending and descending on it. And, behold, the Lord stood above it" (Genesis 28:12–13). This story never spoke to my heart until I stopped seeing a ladder with rungs and pictured a stairway. A ladder seemed so inconsequential for angels and God to ascend and descend upon, or for all mankind to rise upon. There didn't seem to be as much dignity and reverence, but steps rising one after another in solid invitation seemed more fitting for our Creator. Perhaps it is just my own imagination, but the dream held no allure until the ladder became a stairway. And I sincerely believe that is what Jacob saw.

He called the place of his dream *Beth-el*, which means "house of God" (Genesis 28:19*a*). He also called it "the gate of heaven," saying, "Surely the Lord is in this place" (Genesis 28:17, 16). I have never limited the crystal stairs to one aspect of the gospel. That would be folly. Their meaning is in some sense unbounded. But if I were to choose just one, the temple would be it. All that we do in the Lord's House seems so naturally linked to the stairs. Therein we are shown ascending truths, covenants building upon and supporting one another, light upon light, order lifting to order. Through it all, we learn to form the five great unities of oneness that are the answer to Jesus' prayer that we be one as He and His Father are one, and which engage so much of our journey to happiness. We are taught there the meaning of Enoch's Zion, whose people were described as being of "one heart and one mind" (Moses 7:18). Think of the temple's power, for instance, in teaching us to bind spirits together—husband and wife; parent and child; each of us to the other as God's offspring; the living to the dead through countless generations; and each child to his or her Father in Heaven, all humanity to God. This last is beautifully and intimately taught at the crowning moment of the endowment, just as we enter into the celestial world. Oneness will be achieved if we climb to the top of the stairs. That is one of their great purposes.

Within temple walls, I spent the happiest day of my life— the sealing day that united my wife, Laurie, and me together for eternity. That was a climbing day! *United*, *joined*, *married*, even *sealed*, seems an insufficient description for that day and that house. I feel Laurie in every cell. There is not a place within me that she does not fill, and it began on the Lord's stairway of love. On that stairway, imperfect human seedling love started on its journey to become love such as God possesses. It was a summit day for my mortal journey, my highest earthly reach, though I did not know this until she passed away. I always wanted to climb the crystal stairs, but the desire was just that, a desire—fervent, it is true—but not yet reaching the boundaries of absolute need. Now it has become a necessity for me, for only at the top of the stairs will I find her again.

There, too, we will find our Father in Heaven and His Son. The joy of reunion with the Father and Son will culminate in adoration, not just gratitude. But Laurie is the only non-imagined reality I know. I have never seen God. I have never seen Christ—at least not in mortality, so there is no holding place in my memory. So my need to find and climb the true stairway is foremost in my mind. My awareness of that need is not desperate, not anxious, but it does carry an intensity of focus I have never known. It is Jacob's Stairway we want; we must not be diverted by the stairways of men.

GOLD OR STUBBLE?

Even when people have found the true stairway, they have a tendency to want to remodel it to their own specifications. I wish I was free of this tendency. There are times, I'm afraid, when I offer God my own blueprints for stairway alterations. Paul spent most of his life fighting this degenerative impulse in the early Church. More than once he compared the Saints to a building—both collectively and individually. The symbolism of human construction, including tools and buildings, figures very highly in our own faith, finding even a dominant position in the symbolism of the temple. "Ye are God's building," Paul testified. "According to the grace of God which is given unto me, as a wise masterbuilder, I have laid the foundation, and another buildeth thereupon. But let every man take heed how he buildeth thereupon" (1 Corinthians 3:9–10). In Corinth, various teachers had arisen who were teaching doctrines and behaviors inconsistent with the gospel, and they were gaining disciples. Paul compared the philosophies and "wisdom" of men to various building materials which could be added to the foundation of truth he had laid when he introduced the Corinthians to the Savior. The image he wanted us to picture was a beautiful Greek temple. "Now if any man build upon this foundation gold, silver, precious stones, wood, hay, stubble; every man's work shall be made manifest: for the day shall declare it" (1 Corinthians 3:12–13).

Gold or precious stones would endure the tests and trials of life where wood or stubble would not. In our world, every day we encounter "gold morality" and "stubble morality." There are "precious stones ethics and values" as well as "barn wood ethics and values." There is the eternal and the fashionable. We must choose. "It shall be revealed by fire," Paul asserts—the fire of living, of applying the teachings to experience. Only truth endures, no matter how appealing falsehood is dressed. Package your own ideas in whatever wrapping you like, disguise them, fool yourself or others, pretend they mark progress, or that they appeal to the spirit of the age, but still, time is a great revealer. Even if your stairway is made of stone, the eternal ticking of the clock will wear it away. It is crystal we seek.

"Know ye not that ye are the temple of God," Paul continues, "and that the Spirit of God dwelleth in you? If any man defile the temple of God, him shall God destroy; for the temple of God is holy, which temple ye are" (1 Corinthians 3:16–17). We have quoted this for so long, assuming Paul was speaking of the physical body, that it is difficult to read it in the context in which it is found. Paul is speaking of the temple of the entire church, the doctrinal edifice, the community of Saints, or, if we wish to apply it personally, the temple of our mind and testimony. His main thesis does not concern what we would call Word of Wisdom or chastity issues. Rather, the mind and soul are what he is writing about. What ideas, doctrines, morals, ambitions, purposes, teachings, and values are we allowing into the temple of our faith? Barn wood may be lovely in its own right for homey decoration, but it is not consistent with the marble pillars of a Greek temple. And Paul would have us thinking about a beautifully balanced, properly proportioned temple made of the very best materials.

Here is where our imagination must picture what Paul is describing. Whenever we hear newly blazoned "truths" announced before us, we need to pause and ask ourselves if they are consistent with the moral beauty of what Christ taught and how He lived. I try to see the texture and shape of them in comparison. Are these new truths made of gold and granite or of hay and sticks? Will they match the undiminishing eternal radiance of the crystal stairs or would they match the slow but relentless wearing away of stone, brick, or wood inherent in the stairs of men? Are they fit for a temple—or a garage? If we make steps from them, will they lift us higher? "Let no man deceive himself," Paul concludes (1 Corinthians 3:18). This is more likely to happen when we have spent a good deal of time constructing our own stairs or working on the stairways scattered across the plain. Our investment being great, the commitment of time and soul and effort is difficult to walk away from or remove. We may defend our own choices because they are our own, even when we know instinctively that they are not adequate or right.

LEHI'S CHALLENGE TO THE STAIR BUILDERS

The scriptures, prophets, and seers have been given to help us perceive the weaknesses and temporal nature of the stairways of men—to determine what is marble and what is barn wood. An example may be helpful. I have read and taught 2 Nephi 2 for years. It is Lehi's last great doctrinal explication of the Fall and Atonement and man's opportunity to learn the lessons of life and return to our Father in Heaven. In this chapter, a very wise and experienced old man offers the distillation of a lifetime of understanding. During my schooling at the University of Colorado, which has a reputation for its liberal views, I was confronted with positions widely divergent from my own, and I had to sort through them. Some of these stairways I had barely encountered before. We cannot just turn away when challenged. We'll be stronger if we reason and wrestle. I recall many discussions with those committed to various other stairways on the plain. At that time, I reread these familiar verses in 2 Nephi and saw Lehi answering some of the philosophies of men that so tightly grip the thinking and attitudes of our day, and a measure of clarification came. It was only later that I saw Lehi's last words as commenting on the stairs of the plain. They then took on a new meaning.

"Does life really have a purpose?" some ask. "Or do we just exist?" For many, the answer to those questions becomes the pursuit of pleasure and comfort, the accumulation of possessions, and the avoidance of pain. "There are no absolute values, morals, or ethics," another asserts. "Society establishes these things. Everything is relative." "Genetics and environment determine most of what we are. This is the way I am and I can't change—accept it." I met all these philosophies in Colorado—the existentialist, the hedonist, the relativist, the determinist, as well as others. Lehi replies to all these stairways of men. God does have "eternal purposes in the end of man," he wrote (2 Nephi 2:15).

Existence is more than itself. We are moving in a deliberate direction. Most Latter-day Saints have memorized the verse that tells us what those purposes are and what direction we pursue: "Men are, that they might have joy" (2 Nephi 2:25). It is that straightforward. We exist for happiness, joy, gladness, fulfillment. One voice says, "Yes, we agree about happiness being our desire, but pleasure, material things, avoiding discomfort is happiness." Lehi responds that this is not happiness. "If there be no righteousness there be no happiness" (2 Nephi 2:13). Once again, we hear a plain and unadorned truth stated in stark simplicity. We know that happiness is the purpose of existence and we know what happiness is. It is righteousness. Even my young ward member knew this. Mormon theology is clear and cogent. Alma taught, "Do not suppose, because it has been spoken concerning restoration, that ye shall be restored from sin to happiness. Behold, I say unto you, wickedness never was happiness" (Alma 41:10).

Another voice adds, "Ah, but what is righteousness when all things are relative? There are no eternal laws of behavior. *We* decide these things and they change from age to age and society to society." To the relativist, Lehi says, "Men are instructed sufficiently that they know good from evil. And the law is given unto men. . . . If ye shall say there is no law, ye shall also say there is no sin. If ye shall say there is no sin, ye shall also say there is no righteousness" (2 Nephi 2:5, 13). The stairway of relativism will, in the end, destroy our ability to make any moral or ethical judgment whatsoever. Perceiving right and wrong may at times be difficult, but to assume relativity is the answer eliminates the very question itself.

Now a third voice speaks, that of the determinist: "Even if law is absolute and relativism wrong, our fates are determined. We can't really choose to obey your moral law or not." In response, Lehi divides all creation into two categories—things that act and things that are acted upon. He then strongly asserts that man is *not* a thing that is acted upon—he is not determined. "God gave unto man that he should act for himself. . . . They have become free forever, knowing good from evil; to act for themselves and not to be acted upon. . . . And they are free to choose liberty . . . or to choose captivity" (2 Nephi 2:16, 26–27).

Lehi's words are powerful—*act, free, choose.* This truth becomes critical, for instance, for someone with same-sex attraction or with a difficult past that they may use to explain, or, in some cases, justify current behavior. We must look for the stairway that asserts: "The purpose of life is joy and happiness, goodness, virtue, and righteousness." Righteousness is living in accordance with eternal laws which do not change from society to society or religion to religion. Those laws have been taught, though sometimes obscured or misapplied. Men and women were created as creatures that act for themselves. They may choose. They are free. They don't need to let the vicissitudes of life determine what they think or how they will respond. I repeat: the theology is clear and coherent. Lehi also adds the hope that, for those who believe and strive to live well yet fail, a Savior will come and "make intercession for all the children of men" (2 Nephi 2:9).

All of the manmade stairways Lehi addresses do have some reason and validity behind them. We cannot dismiss some degree of relativity in human behavior or that some paths seem to be determined. For many, just existing is a sufficient challenge. That is one of the reasons the stairways of men are so appealing: they do have truth, but the balance is not plumb—it tips in the direction of the favored philosophy, just as politics do. The stairway that will reach to heaven must contain all the steps in harmony. One consistent problem of manmade stairways is the human tendency to privilege one virtue or idea above all others, each step reflecting the same view identical to the one below; one color on the spectrum of truth overpowering all others into its own hue. Often this is done for self-justifying reasons, or mark-missing zeal. We will see, that for a stairway to rise high enough to leave the plain behind, it must envelop and circumscribe all verities, all aspects of human reality, all goodness, all beauty—every color dominant in its own place in truth's spectrum.

"CLEAVETH . . . RECEIVETH . . . EMBRACETH . . . LOVETH"

God has placed an internal compass within us that, if followed, will draw us steadily towards the crystal stairs and away from the stairways of men. In fact, we are ourselves literally that compass. As explained earlier, Doctrine and Covenants 93 teaches that we are beings of light, truth, intelligence, glory—gods in embryo, if you like. Remove this physical exterior and a being of brightness resides within. Even Yoda got it right when he told Luke Skywalker, "Luminous beings are we; not this crude matter."[1]

In Doctrine and Covenants 88, we are taught something powerful about the nature of light and goodness; its nature is to attract more light and goodness. Like invites like. That is why it is inherent and natural for us to climb. "For intelligence cleaveth unto intelligence; wisdom receiveth wisdom; truth embraceth truth; virtue loveth virtue; light cleaveth unto light" (D&C 88:40). The verbs in this verse are wonderful. You and I, as creatures of intelligence and virtue—beings of light and spirit—will *cleave, receive, embrace*, and *love* intelligence, light, and virtue. We are also taught that the natural man is an enemy to God; we will be drawn downward in proportion to the measure we allow it—but I cannot help but believe that virtue, light, and wisdom are commensurately more powerful. Children are born in innocence and goodness, as D&C 93 asserts. They learn their opposites through environment, hence the need to lead them toward the stairway of God as quickly as we can. When I worry about my children and grandchildren, I remind myself often that something consistent with the very highest and most refined within them will draw them to the right stairway. We must draw them into the circle of its beauty and let the stairs work their magic. If not, the stairways of men will become their focus.

CHAPTER THREE

THE CRYSTAL STAIRS AND THE STAIR BUILDER

While ye have light,
Believe in the light,
That ye may be
The children of light.

—JOHN 12:36

"A SEA OF GLASS MINGLED WITH FIRE"

In the Book of Revelation, John saw "a sea of glass like unto crystal" lying before the throne of the Father (Revelation 4:6). Later he returned to this image to give encouragement: "And I saw as it were a sea of glass mingled with fire: and them that had gotten the victory . . . stand on the sea of glass" (Revelation 15:2). In the last chapters of Revelation, John was shown the Celestial City "and the street of the city was pure gold, as it were transparent glass" (Revelation 21:21). This imagery was important enough that Joseph Smith asked the Lord for clarification. In fact, the very first question about Revelation's many symbols was the meaning of the "sea of glass spoken of by John." Joseph was answered it was "the earth, in its sanctified, immortal, and eternal state" (D&C 77:1). In a later revelation, Joseph Smith returned to the crystal imagery, adding, "The angels . . . reside in the presence of God, on a globe like a sea of glass and fire. . . . The place where God resides is a great Urim and Thummim. This earth, in its sanctified and immortal state, will be made like unto crystal and will be a Urim and Thummim to the inhabitants who dwell thereon" (D&C 130:6–9). *Urim* is the Hebrew plural for light. It literally means "lights," and light is intrinsically interchangeable with truth. *Thummim* is the plural for perfection—"perfections."

There is an inseparable relationship taught in the scriptures between light and perfection or truth and goodness. We are offered the opportunity of climbing above the wasteland on a stairway of truth and purity and perfection—truth in all the varied hues and colors of God's eternal spectrum. This leads to and generates, in those who draw it into themselves, all goodness, all perfections, all the qualities of godliness, especially as those perfections were manifested to the world through the life and teachings of Jesus of Nazareth. Each step—each holy and pure truth—is unique, varied in distinctive beauty, begetting goodness, and inviting all to climb. They can, indeed, draw all things into their own perfect state—certainly including you and me.

A stair has a vertical riser and a horizontal tread upon which to stand. On the crystal stairs, this translates to a unique combination of the purity of truth and the perfection of goodness. When we internalize truth—when we love it—it brings about a refinement in our nature. It awakens and stimulates the natural goodness that constitutes the core of our being. That is why Abraham, a stranger and pilgrim, desired knowledge. He knew what it would do for his character and disposition. He opened his own autobiographical story in the Pearl of Great Price with this aspiration: "Having been myself a follower of righteousness, desiring also to be one who possessed great knowledge, and to be a greater follower of righteousness, and to possess a greater knowledge" (Abraham 1:2). It is the key to everything we know about him and the force that moved his life forward toward exaltation. The Savior also followed this pattern of the two-dimensional nature of the stairs—the vertical riser of truth supporting the horizontal plane, the tread, of goodness; or, as in Abraham's words, knowledge generates righteousness, which generates more knowledge, which generates more desire for righteousness. "That which is of God is light," we are taught, "and he that receiveth light, and continueth in God, receiveth more light; and that light groweth brighter and brighter until the perfect day" (D&C 50:24). The brightness of truth leads to the perfect day of eternal goodness of soul.

KNOWING HOW TO WORSHIP

Doctrine and Covenants 93 begins with the Savior's affirmation that He is "the true light that lighteth every man that cometh into the world" (D&C 93:2). He is the example. We follow Him up the stairway. For much of the remainder of D&C 93, He helps us understand that climbing the stairway is a "grace for grace" endeavor. He "came and . . . dwelt among us," but "he received not of the fulness at the first, but received grace for grace; and he received not of the fulness at first, but continued from grace to grace, until he received a fulness; and thus he was called the Son of God, because he received not of the fulness at the first" (D&C 93:11–14).

John the Baptist's witness was restored by the Prophet in D&C 93: "I, John, bear record that he received a fulness of the glory of the Father; and he received all power" (D&C 93:16–17).

When I first comprehended the truth of John's witness, the very words created the image of the crystal stairway once again in my mind. Each step is a level of grace acquired by the Savior one by one, higher and higher, until all the fulness of the Father's glory, light, and power was His. But this was not a state He attained at once. Each level of perfected purity built upon its predecessor in a natural progression. Every act of obedience brought greater light and truth, which was welcomed by continued obedience and righteousness—grace for grace. All truths leading to all perfections! "He that keepeth his commandments receiveth truth and light, until he is glorified in truth" (D&C 93:28).

The Savior's own ascent was given to us "that you may understand and know how to worship, and know what you worship, that you may come unto the Father in my name, and in due time receive of his fulness. For if you keep my commandments you shall receive of his fulness . . . I say unto you, you shall receive grace for grace" (D&C 93:19–20). Here is the Savior's invitation to climb as He did. Worship is not just hymns, or sacrament meetings, or temple sessions. That is only a small part of it. It is *living* as Christ did, one stair at a time, adding each quality and perfection of His nature to our own. We worship a being who climbed the stairway, grace for grace, into Godhood's exaltation and fulness. When we do the same, we are worshipping in the way God most desires. We also follow His path knowing that "in due time" may be a distant future and so we must be patient with ourselves and each other. Joseph Smith's words so testified when he wrote: "When you climb up a ladder, you must begin at the bottom, and ascend step by step, until you arrive at the top; and so it is with the principles of the Gospel—you must begin with the first, and go on until you learn all the principles of salvation. But it will be a great while after you have passed through the veil before you will have learned them. It is not all to be comprehended in this world; it will be a great work to learn our salvation and exaltation even beyond the grave."[1] Perhaps what is so remarkable about our Savior's rise from grace to grace into the fulness of the Father was that it reached its fulfillment in this life, while ours will be a more time-expansive journey.

In the meantime, we will follow Christ's invitation given in two early sections of the Doctrine and Covenants: "I [am] in the midst of you. Fear not to do good. . . . Look unto me in every thought; doubt not, fear not" (D&C 6:32–33, 36). "Learn of me, and listen to my words; walk in the meekness of my Spirit, and you shall have peace in me" (D&C 19:23). There are our climbing instructions. We look. We learn. We listen. Then we walk. We don't need theological debates. We don't have to work out rules, ethical theories, or moral lists of laws. We don't, at least not immediately, need to make all the pieces fit. We look, we learn, we listen and then do the best we can to imitate all that He was and did. That is what children do best—they imitate. It is a high degree of worship.

In the scriptures, we are often called the children of Christ, His sons and daughters. Mormon told those struggling to do good that if they persisted they "certainly will be a child of Christ" (Moroni 7:19). The result of following this pattern will be freedom from doubt and fear. We climb with peace. We climb with assurance and a calm soul. We follow Him up the stairway. He has showed us the way. The great Chinese sage Confucius told his followers to learn as if they were following someone whom they had no chance of overtaking, but were afraid to lose sight of. As we stand at the foot of the stairs watching the Stair Builder ascend, this is the desire we have.

ARE THE STAIRS STRONG?

I remember talking to a very learned man, a good man also, who said, "Your beliefs are very comforting, very beautiful—too beautiful for the world in which we live. It is a pretty world you have created with your loving God, His grand plan and promises, but it is not a true one. It does not match reality as most people experience life. The world is suffering. It is brutal; it is fear; it is poverty, hunger, war, disease, and death. Besides, to explain away evil in the world because some woman ate a piece of fruit paints a pretty unpleasant picture of a good God, don't you think?" I had no answer. I was too young and inexperienced. In essence, he did not believe the stairs could hold the reality of our world. His view is that they will shatter.

Are the stairs strong? It is a legitimate question. Will they truly hold our lives, hopes, dreams, and possibilities? And if they are that strong—those radiant, pure, love-filled truths from the bosom of God Himself—are we even capable of climbing them? My learned friend described the world as many people experience it. So is exaltation only for the deeply diligent, faith-gifted few, or is it really possible for each of us to climb the stairs of light?

The Lord said His stairs are strong. He told us we may climb them. Did He mean we should only make the *attempt*, or that we had every hope of succeeding, that we could do it? Has God made the bar too high, and are most of us then doomed to the guilt—mild or crippling—of constant failure? Doctrine and Covenants 76, speaking of the telestial glory, says: "But behold, and lo, we saw the glory and the inhabitants of the telestial world, that they were as innumerable as the stars in the firmament of heaven, or as the sand upon the seashore" (D&C 76:109). What are we to do with that knowledge? The stairs of men could not deliver the highest happiness, but they were climbable. How do we reconcile a God of light and love with the brutal realities of life as so very many people experience it? Can we rely on all of those lovely truths with their accompanying perfections of character—bright, golden light, hope-filled promises—and can we live them? Will they bear us up in a mortal, fallen world? Will they truly bring happiness, reunion, fulfillment, answers, comfort, courage, and direction sufficient for the suffering, disappointment, cruelty, seemingly senseless pain, waste, and death we see all around us? It is a question I ponder often with only faith to reassure.

So what do we do? We climb, for that is all we can do. We follow, because there is really no other choice. We live the life the Savior offers and then we will see if the stairs can bear the pressures of mortality. It is not a question of debate, philosophy, or theological discussion. Will happiness, in spite of all the opposition that life can array against us, still be the outcome? Choose anything the Savior asks you and me to do—do it and see what follows. This is true even if you don't believe. Act on the light! Embrace the truths! Then assess what perfections have been created. What does the world look like now? The stairs *will* hold!

I suppose some may feel I am evading the question. Perhaps it is the only answer with which I am comfortable. We will leave the deep discussions to the debaters and instead be about our "father's business" (Luke 2:49). We will feed His lambs and His sheep because we love Him *and* them (see John 21:15–17). We will treat the "least of these my brethren" as we would treat Christ Himself—giving meat to the hungry, drink to the thirsty, welcoming the stranger, clothing the naked, and visiting the imprisoned, whether those needs be physical or spiritual. (See Matthew 25:35–36, 40.) We will run to the returning prodigal with shoes for his feet and a ring for his finger (see Luke 15:11–32). We will say to the fallen, "Neither do I condemn thee: go, and sin no more" (John 8:11). We will heal, within the limits of our own possibilities, the wounds and sicknesses with which a soul may be burdened. We will render unto Caesar, drop our mites into the treasury, and leave all, even when the nets are full. The world will find us peacemakers, meek, merciful, and hungering after righteousness. We will turn to the little ones with an inviting voice and "suffer the little children to come unto [Him], and forbid them not" (Mark 10:14). We will pray, "Father, forgive them; for they know not what they do" (Luke 23:34). And we will say in all things, certainly in the most difficult, dark nights of our Gethsemanes, "Nevertheless not my will, but thine, be done" (Luke 22:42).

Only when we have done these things will we know the true strength of the crystal stairs and the wisdom and goodness of the Stair Builder. When we have done these things, we will not think His way does not take reality into account nor sufficiently meet the challenges of our world or of our individual lives. When we have looked and learned and listened and walked, climbing grace for grace, we will not be tempted to leave and try the stairways of men.

We can wrestle with theology, doctrines, the weaknesses of leaders, or we can love. The answer may be that simple, that plain. There is cruelty—let us not be cruel. There is greed and selfishness—let us not seek our own. There is enmity and anger—let us not retaliate nor hate. There is domination and tyranny—let us love and sacrifice. This is what Christ came to teach, not only by voice, but by His very life. He lived a perfect, loving life in a world of darkest opposition. "The prince of this world cometh, and hath nothing in me," the Savior said (John 14:30). As we strive to say those words of ourselves, His truth and His love can be stronger than all that is dark, for "in him was life; and the life was the light of men. And the light shineth in darkness; and the darkness comprehended it not" (John 1:4–5).

If the Savior could climb the stairs, we must believe that we can also. Peter impossibly walked on the water because Jesus did. "I am the light of the world: he that followeth me shall not walk in darkness, but shall have the light of life" (John 8:12). How great that darkness seems at times in a world that has produced the Holocaust, the Cambodian killing fields, and the Sandy Hook shooting. Yet we can love even the ugly and the hateful, "because the darkness is past, and the true light now shineth" (1 John 2:8). The stairs under His loving footsteps could bear the weight of all the sins, suffering, and tragedy of the world.

Fyodor Dostoyevsky, a man of tremendous faith, but also a man who wrestled deeply with the suffering of the world, once wrote: "I have composed within myself a confession of faith, . . . in which everything is clear and holy for me. This confession is very simple . . . to believe that there is nothing more beautiful, more profound, more sympathetic, more reasonable, more manly, and more perfect than Christ. . . . Furthermore, if anyone proved to me that Christ was outside the truth, and it really was a fact that the truth was outside of Christ, I would rather remain with Christ than with the truth."[2] Let us live a life like Christ lived, for we will find nothing purer, more goodness-infused, or radiant with the spectrum of God's light.

The question of the stairs' strength and the need to follow the Stair Builder has taken on a much more intense meaning for me now. If the stairs are just glass—fragile and incapable of holding, of explaining, of bringing sense to even the harshest of earth's realities—then I have truly lost my wife Laurie to cancer and nothing else really matters. Macbeth would then be proved right: "Life's but a walking shadow; a poor player that struts and frets his hour upon the stage, and then is heard no more. It is a tale told by an idiot, full of sound and fury, signifying nothing."[3] How can we possibly come to that conclusion? Or are the stairs the true reality, the strongest thing we can ever behold, because the Stair Builder was not only their creator, but the first to climb their heights? Paul testified we must progress, "looking unto Jesus the author and finisher of our faith" (Hebrews 12:2). Somehow, with our vision focused on Him, all the rest become ever-diminishing distractions to the grand obsession of life—climbing!

CHAPTER FOUR

SHATTERING
THE STAIRS

Let us lay aside every weight,
And the sin which doth so easily beset us,
And let us run with patience the race that is set before us,
Looking unto Jesus the author and finisher of our faith;
Who for the joy that was set before him
Endured.

—HEBREWS 12:1–2

TO KEEP OR TO CLIMB

I think some of the most difficult choices I have seen people
wrestle tenaciously with is the decision to climb or to keep
those weaknesses that hold them back. I, too, have struggled with
keep-or-climb battles. But I do not get the impression that the
Lord is expecting perfection before the upward journey begins;
rather, we need to be unburdened of personal weight we have
accumulated so that our ascent may be easier. He would have us
leave the negatives, the distractions, that we might acquire the
positives more readily.

I have loved for years a statement by C. S. Lewis about the

number of chances God will give us. "I believe," he wrote, "that if a million chances were likely to do good, they would be given."[1] I believe this too with all my heart. Failure does not bring condemnation, but renewed invitation. When we turn back to the stairs with a renewed desire to climb, we can be assured of the words spoken by the compassionate father of the prodigal son, who "ran, and fell on his neck, and kissed him."

"This my son was dead, and is alive again; he was lost, and is found" (Luke 15:20, 24). It is an ever-echoing summons to try again.

How often did the Savior help a willing but oh-so-human Peter to part with what held him back? Those frequent moments have endeared Peter to me and can help us understand why Jesus chose him to lead. He took rebuke meekly and desired to part with all that held him back so that he could follow his Master in the upward journey to godliness. Yet in his thrice-repeated denial of the Savior, Peter had to face his own overconfident assessment, his touch of unseen pride. It was perhaps a weakness that was also evidenced in a bit of condescending judgment of the other disciples when Peter said, "Though *all* men shall be offended because of thee, yet will I *never*" (Matthew 26:33; emphasis added). I have found that "all/never" statements often return to teach us humility.

When James and John wanted to sit on the Savior's right and left side, was His mild and gentle rebuke not a kind urging to conquer ambition and their natural-man desire for precedence? (See Mark 10:35–45.) These same two disciples, ready to call down fire from heaven upon the Samaritans for rejecting their Lord, had to leave behind their prejudices and intolerance, that self-righteous indignation that is so unfortunately pleasing to the human mind and that finds justification in misplaced zeal. It is not too much love of God that is the problem, but too little love of mankind. "Ye know not what manner of spirit ye are of," Jesus told them (Luke 9:55).

The scriptures are filled, cover to cover, with great men and women looking into their own bundles and bags and then parting, out of love for the Lord, with those things that hold them back. We watch Nephi crying, "O wretched man that I am." As I have read this over the years, it seems to me he is concerned that he gave in to anger and a little self-pity (2 Nephi 4:17, 26–27).

We have sometimes judged harshly the rich young ruler, but he only lacked "one thing." I have not yet reached the point where just one thing remains in my suitcase. And we read specifically that, "Jesus beholding him loved him" (Mark 10:21). We need to know, as we fight to part with what we carry, that Jesus beholding us loves us also. There is encouragement in that thought.

Many times, in the mission field or while serving as a bishop, I watched others struggle to part with the bundles of past habits, attitudes, behaviors, or possessions. I remember a beloved French family whose father fought the demon of tobacco and won, because the pull of the stairs and their Builder was stronger in his heart than a lifelong habit. He went on to become a Church leader and build up branches in several cities in which he lived. I remember also those who failed to put away their baggage and turned to climb other stairways. One of my saddest moments as a bishop occurred when I could not give a temple recommend to a mother and father to watch their daughter be married in the temple because they had not come to church in years nor paid their tithing. They attended for a month, gave me one tithing envelope and wanted the recommend. I tried to explain, but was met with fury and a slammed door. Later, at their house, I was driven off the front lawn with the garden hose. That was the lowest moment of a five-year service. Had it been my church, I would have given the recommend to them to avoid contention, but as I had to remind myself frequently, "It's not your church, Mike." They are still climbing the stairways of men, and in their minds, it is my fault.

There was another family, active in every sense of the word except tithing. There were too many things they wanted and the budget was empty on Sunday mornings. I loved them too and often asked the Lord, "For them, can't we just waive the commandment?" While I also knew they spent more on entertainment than on building the kingdom, it did not change my concern or desires for them. If I, human as anyone on earth, could feel such affection for them, how much more did God? Sadly, they too have now left the stairs.

There are men I love as dearly as any brother who choose not to climb because they are nursing a past offense and can't let it go, or holding on to some rag of resentment or limiting habit. The heavy weight of pornography rests in too many backpacks and suitcases. Some carry hate, or fear, or prejudice, or greed, or covetousness—all tiring and arduous loads to lift. For one friend of my youth it was long hair. Such a sad, silly thing, really. For another, a genre of music held such power. I have tried not to judge others. Because judging—measuring our brothers' and sisters' bundles—is a weight all its own. I have my own goodbyes to say as I inventory the burdens I still carry. So now when I return to the image in my mind of those travelers who depart the stairs, their bags and boxes still clutched in their hands, I feel a great loss and deep sympathy. The stairways of men will, in all probability, allow them to hold the weights they cherish, but I don't think the happiness of lesser heights, constantly adapting and rebuilding, will ever begin to compensate for the feel of the delicately etched prisms of glass beneath one's feet—standing on pure truth and feeling the growing goodness inside—nor the sight of the Stair Builder's figure ever-present before us as we follow. In these examples, please realize I am not simply talking about remaining active in the Church. The stairs are so much more than that.

Jesus taught that we had to lose ourselves in order to find ourselves. I suppose a focus on self is inherent in every traveler's bag. To view life through a selfish lens will always cause a distortion. We perceive both our own reflection and that of others "through a glass, darkly" (1 Corinthians 13:12). I believe the heaviest and most difficult weight to leave behind is our own sense of self, our ego. Ultimately, if we are to climb, we will need to free ourselves of ourselves. I wish I could tell you how to do this, but I am a long way from mastering my own desires and inward turning to the self. We gain a heavy weight in our bags when we ungraciously separate ourselves from other selves, when we view the differences between us and place a value in our favor. However, the recognition of the need to forget the self is opening the lid of our most cherished suitcase and is a beginning.

Threads and Shoelaces

One of the greatest examples to inspire us to empty our suitcases is Abraham. When his brother-in-law Lot was captured in a raid upon Sodom, Abraham went to his rescue. What Lot was doing in Sodom is a lesson in itself, but in his rescue Abraham freed all the other captive citizens of Sodom. He also "brought back all the goods" of Sodom. (Genesis 14:16). He was met by Sodom's king with an interesting proposition. "Give me the persons, and take the goods to thyself." His response is most instructive: "And Abram said to the king of Sodom, I have lift up mine hand unto the Lord, the most high God, . . . that I will not take from a thread even to a shoelatchet, and that I will not take anything that is thine" (Genesis 14:21–22). Abraham wanted nothing from Sodom (or from the world, which Sodom has represented since the time of Genesis). A thread is a tiny thing, as is a shoelace. What is a thread's worth of dishonesty? What is a thread's worth of immodesty or questionable entertainment? What is a thread's worth of the world? I do not presume to know the answer for others (or even myself); we do not wish to strain at gnats, either. As in all things there must be balance, but Abraham's decision, his attitude toward compromise in areas of integrity, is remarkably instructive.

Abraham's rejection of the thread and the shoelace stands before us as a sentinel of goodness, a standard we can aim for. How much lighter he climbed, and thus how much more quickly! I used to teach this lesson in a dark blue suit. Before the class began, I would place a single white thread on the lapel, then wait and watch for the reaction. I could tell in my students' eyes and expressions that they were bothered by that single thread. Eventually someone would raise his or her hand and draw my attention to it. Sometimes someone near the back of the class would catch my eye and brush their lapel silently to let me know I had something on it. I would look down and say, "Oh, it's just a tiny white thread," and continue teaching. I couldn't do so for long, however, because soon no one was listening anymore—they were all staring at that obnoxious thread. I don't claim to know what a thread's worth of the world looks like on a Latter-day Saint, but I sense it is distracting. I sometimes wonder how many of my own threads are on display—threads I would want to remove if I was more aware.

THE "HARD SAYINGS"

When laboring to part with my own "things of this world," or when helping others set aside what they still carry, I have found encouragement and comfort in Peter's words to Jesus at a time when many of Christ's followers left Him for the stairs of the world. I love this story for the glimpse of the Savior's soul it gives and for the strength it can bestow.

After having fed the five thousand, Jesus returned to Capernaum. In the synagogue, many of His followers sought Him, but they were more interested, it seems, in the physical bread He could provide than the spiritual truths He had to offer. Had not Moses fed the children of Israel manna in the wilderness for forty years? How could one afternoon and a five-loaf-miracle compare with that? In one of the most masterful discourses in the New Testament, Jesus told them that *He* was the "bread of life," and tried to raise their sights to the spiritual nourishment He so wanted to share. He could not be the kind of Messiah they wanted. He must be the kind they needed, the kind that His Father had taught Him to be. He had something far greater than manna to offer. For many, however, this was too much, as it went against centuries of tradition. "Many . . . of his disciples, when they heard this, said, This is an *hard saying*; who can hear it?" (John 6:60; emphasis added).

We all hear hard sayings in our lives, and they are different for each of us. What is easy for me to understand and believe and do may be difficult for you; likewise in those things that are hard for me but easy for you. We must not judge each other in the "hard sayings" with which we wrestle. "Jesus knew in himself that his disciples murmured at it," and "said unto them, Doth this offend you?" (John 6:61). In John 6, these disciples—and we must remember these are *followers*, not just curious onlookers or skeptics—could not part with the old traditions of what their Messiah would do for them. They could not leave them on the ground and turn to the transparent steps to climb. So they left, like many I saw as I watched in the colored lights of the stairs, for more congenial stairways of the world. "From that time many of his disciples went back, and walked no more with him" (John

6:66). If we visualize this scene, we can almost hear the silence as the synagogue empties, leaving Jesus alone with the twelve apostles and perhaps a few others. There is sorrow in the air and resignation. Then, in one of the most poignant moments in the scriptures, Jesus turns to His twelve chosen disciples and asks, "Will ye also go away?" That is a question we must all answer when we face the hard sayings. "Then Simon Peter answered him, Lord, *to whom shall we go?* thou hast the words of eternal life. And we believe and are sure that thou art that Christ, the Son of the living God" (John 6:67–69; emphasis added).

We must all rise to this moment of commitment if we hope to endure to the end of the stairs. It comes after we have looked, learned, and listened. It comes after we have received the testimony of the Holy Spirit, which Peter did as recorded in Matthew 16. It comes when we truly, deeply realize that there is no other way. "To whom shall we go?" "I am the way, the truth, and the life: no man cometh unto the Father, but by me" (John 14:6). If we think there is another way to the highest happiness, we may seek it among the stairs of men. That can be especially compelling when hard sayings come into our lives, but if we, like Peter, know that His way is the way, that His truth is the truth, that there is no real life without Him, no climb that ascends as high, then we will not be tempted to turn away.

When I served as a stake missionary in Colorado while studying at the university, I became acquainted with a wonderful young African-American student named Charles. He was not affiliated with any particular religion. We became very close friends so it was natural to introduce him to the gospel. He received the missionaries, progressed rapidly, and we had many deep discussions on various topics. He was exceptionally intelligent, easygoing, and a great conversationalist. I loved him thoroughly. The only thing that appeared to stop him was a lack of answers to his prayers. I used to ask him with every conversation if he had prayed and if the Lord had responded. Every session, the answer would be negative. One morning, after several months of friendship and teaching, he came into the office to tell me a story. He prefaced it by saying that he had decided not to join the Church, which distressed me greatly. Then he related the following experience.

"I went into the Flatirons above Boulder yesterday to pray. I knew I had to make a decision, so I asked God what to do. After what seemed a long period, I heard a voice calling my name. 'Charles . . . Charles.'"

He paused at this point and remained silent for a long time. I finally couldn't bear the suspense, so I broke the stillness and asked, "What did you do?"

With great emotion—for this was a struggle—he said, "I got up and ran down the mountain." Then, with a voice nearing desperation, which was unusual for him, seeing the look of puzzlement in my eyes, he said, "Mike, if I joined your church I would be the only black man in the congregation. I don't think I have that much courage in spite of how kind everyone has been. I was afraid of the answer I would get, so I ran." I think of him often. He had so much to offer. I don't know what the Spirit would have said to him. Perhaps something that would have instilled the courage to drop that perception. Perhaps some guidance or direction he could pursue. I believe he sensed the goodness of what he had been taught already. He may not have needed an answer that it was true. But we are never told how the story *could* have ended, only how it did. This was his "hard saying"; it was a hard one indeed and one we all can understand. To this day, my full empathy rests with his decision.

When the hard-saying times come in my own life, when it would be very convenient if the gospel was not true or good, when with relief I could far too easily turn to the manmade stairs that do not require the faith or sacrifice that the thin, glowing steps of glass do, I repeat to myself all the "I am" statements of the Savior. "I am the Bread of Life"; "I am the Rock"; "I am the Good Shepherd"; "I am the Light of the World"; "I am the Living Water"; "I am the True Vine"; "I am the Way"; "I am the Resurrection and the Life." Then I follow each with their unstated assumption—there is no other bread; there is no other rock; there is no other shepherd; there is no other light; there is no other water; there is no other vine, nor way, nor resurrection, nor life.

There is no other stairway that will reach where we want to go. To believe this, to affirm it and to in time be certain of it will bring the courage and faith to leave the bundles, bags, and boxes. To whom else would we go? As my young friend so simply stated: "There is only one way to get to heaven—righteousness." We must decide if that is what we want.

"If You Only Walk Long Enough"

Please understand that the assertion that there is no other stairway is not meant to be exclusionary of other churches or religions. Religion serves to channel human energy and aspirations heavenward and to offer us opportunity to grow spiritually and serve. I believe our Father in Heaven has been directing light and truth and goodness and beauty into the stream of human history in every way He possibly can, through every medium available, and that all the major religions have the potential to put one onto the stairway. Climbing the stairs is the acquiring of character and perfections and godliness such as Christ possessed. Those who cannot hear the voice of a prophet or apostle may hear the voice of a poet or playwright, a sage or artist or philosopher. If not nourished by doctrine, they may be nourished by story or myth. It is our *response* to truth that matters, and how we allow that truth to change and mold our character until we think and believe and forgive and obey and love as Christ does.

"I am the way, the truth, and the life" means, I believe, that Christ's way of living is the only way to a fullness of happiness. Many have taught that way of living—to a degree. They have not all been Christians. Fullness comes when each one of us reaches the highest that is within us, which is very high indeed. For just a moment, forget names and labels, lay aside differences of doctrine and the quarrels that have arisen over it, and focus on Jesus and how He lived and on how all good men lived. We must be like Him, filled with charity, as Paul so movingly and eloquently describes in 1 Corinthians 13—kind, suffering long, envying not, not provoked, thinking no evil, rejoicing in truth, bearing all things, hoping all things, enduring all things. This is how those who leave their packages and suitcases at the foot of the stairway climb, following the Stair Builder upwards. But we will not be able to sustain the effort that climbing that stairway asks of us unless we are absolutely committed to those as the *only* stairs whose top truly reaches heaven and godly happiness. Certainly there are lesser rewards and lesser stairways that you can reach if that is where you wish to go.

There is a marvelous conversation between Alice and the Cheshire Cat in *Alice in Wonderland* that I have turned to it in my life on numerous occasions as a reminder that it *does* matter which stairway I scale and what I must abandon to climb it:

"'Would you tell me, please, which way I ought to go from here?'

"'That depends a good deal on where you want to get to,' said the Cat.

"'I don't much care where—' said Alice.

"'Then it doesn't matter which way you go,' said the Cat.

"'—so long as I get *somewhere*,' Alice added as an explanation.

"'Oh, you're sure to do that,' said the Cat, 'if only you walk long enough.'"[2]

THE LOTA OF WATER

The great danger of the plain, with its multitude of stairways, is thinking that it represents the highest reality or to mistake the process of building other stairs for arriving at their pinnacle, to attach a certain permanency to the constructs of this world—the possessions in our suitcases. As the Christian hymn reminds us, there is "change and decay in all around I see."[3] This is a lovely world; God would have us be happy as mortals, as well as eternally, but the present, the world, can become too dominant in our thinking and control too much of our decision making. One of the qualities that manmade stairways share is their tendency to "move with the times," to be "carried about by every wind of doctrine" (Ephesians 4:14). But we seek the city beyond time.

There is a Hindu parable that has invited me to much meditation and provided me with perspective. It is rather a haunting story, typical of Eastern religions in their ability to move through symbol and suggestion—and somewhat ambiguous. It appeals to my imagination. In Hinduism, the three dominant deities are Brahma, the Creator; Vishnu, the Preserver; and Shiva, the Destroyer (of ignorance and wickedness). Vishnu is deeply loved and comes to earth in diverse forms to save the world when it needs saving. In the parable, a rather unique Hindu sage named Narada is conversing with Vishnu. He is a strange fellow, always asking questions that on the surface aren't too important, but closer examination reveals how penetrating they can be. He carries a sitar with him and lives in Vishnu's heaven. He asks Vishnu, "What is *maya*?" He has heard that the world is *maya*. That is quite a question. There is no sufficient translation for *maya*, nor an explanation that conveys its meaning even in Hinduism. It represents the transitory, illusionary nature of this world, but even that is an incomplete definition. It is difficult for Christians to grasp the concept in religious terms, but that line about change and decay from "Abide with Me!" gives some understanding.

You can't explain *maya*, and the Hindus don't really try—you can only experience it. Vishnu knows this and tells Narada that he can't explain *maya*. Narada threatens to stop worshipping Vishnu if he doesn't get a satisfactory response, so Vishnu promises an answer if Narada will only get him a drink of water from a village in the distance. They have been traveling in a wasted desert land and Vishnu is very thirsty. He sits under a tree in the shade and hands Narada a *lota* (a brass vessel) to bring back the water.

"Do you promise to explain *maya* if I bring back the *lota* filled with water?"

"Yes," answers Vishnu, "I will tell you. I'll wait right here till you return."

The village is only a short way off; Narada will be back in no time at all, less than an hour. When he enters the village, he meets a beautiful young woman. There is something familiar about her. She has Vishnu eyes, serene, knowing, calm.

"I need a *lota* of water," he says. "It is very important!"

She welcomes him into her family hut and disappears into the next room. Narada is impatient. He is on the verge of understanding the nature of the world, of achieving wisdom; eternal answers await him when he brings Vishnu the *lota* of water. "Where is that girl?" he wonders.

Soon her parents appear and offer him a meal. At first he declines, but Indian hospitality demands he partake and he is haunted by the girl's face and wants to see her again. He eats, gets tired, and is invited to stay the night. He knows he must get back to Vishnu, but the eternal questions can wait till morning.

You can guess the rest of the story—one thing leads to another, days go by. He marries the girl and takes over the family property when his in-laws die. Children are born. He becomes an important man in the village. His responsibilities and possessions grow. At the back of his mind he remembers Vishnu sitting under the tree in the desert not too far away, but his once-urgent need to understand *maya* lessens, leaving him with only a vague and occasional uneasiness, soon dismissed when the important affairs of his life press for his attention. Still—Vishnu is waiting.

Then the floods come. The floods always come. That is a reality of life. We all face floods of various strengths and destruction. Narada is swept into the water. His home, his land, all his belongings wash away in the brown surging river. He reaches for his wife and children, but is swallowed up in the swirling water and passes into unconsciousness. When he awakes, he is lying comfortably on the ground, his head cradled in the lap of Vishnu, who is looking into his face with compassion—a tranquil, calm, untroubled, peaceful smile on his face. You see that smile on statues and art all over Asia. It is also the smile of Siddhartha, who became the Buddha.

"Do you now understand what *maya* is?" Vishnu asks.

Narada is still a bit confused. "Have you been here all this time?"

"Yes," Vishnu replies, "But the wait was not long."

"Don't tell me that none of that happened," Narada replies. "It was real. I've been gone years. I was an important man. I was married, I had children, I owned land, possessions."

"But you wanted to know what *maya* is," Vishnu says. "Do you now know?"

That parable may clarify things for you, or it may make no sense at all. It is Hindu in tone. It helped me understand something of life when I first read it many, many years ago. It has stayed with me all this time. How grateful we are that we know family is an everlasting thing, but it's important to remember that it is only available at the top of the stairs. Part of walking "the path of the low valley" (2 Nephi 4:32) is gaining discernment, knowing that the floods will come, but also knowing in time we will end up back in the lap of Vishnu. In the meantime, let us try not to become too attached to temporal things at the expense of understanding eternal ones, to keeping instead of climbing. Within the compass of this parable, that is to live in illusion.

CHAPTER FIVE

CLIMBING THE
CRYSTAL STAIRS

Give unto the Lord the glory due unto his name:
Bring an offering, and come before him:
Worship the Lord in the beauty of holiness.

—1 CHRONICLES 16:29

BEING AND BECOMING

We have arrived at the most critical juncture of our story. Exactly what does it mean to climb the crystal stairs? I felt in my early reflections that the stairs were things I had to *do*, not qualities I needed to *acquire*. If I did the correct things like paying my tithing, or saying my prayers, or reading my scriptures, or fulfilling my callings, or going to the temple, or serving my mission, I would be climbing off the wasteland and into the clouds. These are all important; I wish to take nothing from them, but they are not important in themselves, as checks on a long to-do list. By doing them, we only climb if we allow what we're doing

59

to change our souls, to make us more Christlike, more like the Father. I believe this is what Jesus meant when He said, "Many will say to me in that day, Lord, Lord, have we not . . . in thy name done many wonderful works?" But the Savior will profess, "I never knew you" (Matthew 7:22–23). That is why it may be possible for a godly Catholic or Buddhist to be higher on the stairway than a Latter-day Saint, depending on the quality of soul he or she is developing. In this sense, the crystal stairs are not specifically about religions. In other words, I believe that all religions may get one onto the stairway.

How high one can climb will depend on the inspiration and opportunity presented by one's chosen faith (and a claimed faith is better than no faith) and one's response to offered truth. Obviously, the more truth we're given, the higher our potential to climb becomes. As Latter-day Saints, we affirm that we have heaven-reaching light to bestow—goodness and understanding and encouragement in some of its most mature forms. That is what the Sacred Grove was all about. The highest truths can lead to the highest perfections. But that expectation of eventual perfection must not stop us from enjoying the gladness of simple goodness. And while perfection must not rob unadorned decency of its luster, nonetheless we desire to climb.

I don't recall when I fully realized that *climbing* equaled *becoming*, and that we are limited only by our own choices in the qualities of godliness we can develop. For example, forgiveness is certainly one of the most beloved and radiant of all the steps on the stairway. Yet I have often stood paralyzed before this particular step because I would not let go of the sickly-sweet savor of bitterness or self-pity that comes when we have been badly hurt by another and hold onto resentment. However, we must learn to do so, because we must learn to do all things well until we can say, as did Jesus, "For I do always those things that please him" (John 8:29).

I could never reconcile within my own mind and heart the idea that we do all we can and then the Savior will do the rest. Some have suggested—at times rather uncharitably—that I don't believe in Christ enough. That may certainly be true. My faith is undoubtedly lacking and needs strengthening with higher hope, but I don't think I can love my Savior more intensely than I do, at least within the limits of mortal knowledge. I have always loved Him, and loved Him deeply. I admit that the Atonement is beyond my comprehension, but I don't see Him lifting me over any of the stairs. All our failures at becoming he will forgive freely, and joyfully, and delightedly, but sooner or later, in this life or the next, we will find ourselves like Christ and the Father or we will become satisfied with another level of happiness. This is a gospel of happiness, and all kingdoms of glory are places of joy, but if we continue the climb to the top, with Christ's ever-present example and mercy to lead us, we will in time live and be as He is. That is what the stairs are all about.

When I chose the chairman for my doctoral committee, he called me into his office for an initial orientation meeting. We were very different in personality and beliefs, but I will never forget how good he made me feel when he said: "You will receive your PhD! You will pass the final defense because I will not let you into that room until I know absolutely that you will succeed. So you may enter with complete confidence. Further, I will not stop working with you and helping you until you attain that point. The only thing that can stop you is your own desire to quit. I can't help you with that, but as long as you will work and learn and study, your PhD is assured. So relax and enjoy the experience without anxiety."

It seems that our Savior says a similar thing to us all. We need not overly worry about the judgment. We will, as we are told, one day stand before the bar of God, but I believe we will not make our defense until we and our Lord are absolutely satisfied that we will hear those peace-giving words, "Well done, my good and faithful servant," or perhaps, "This is my beloved child, in whom I am well pleased." The last verses in the Book of Mormon suggest that to me. We will "meet . . . before the pleasing bar of the great Jehovah," and we will meet there "triumphant" (Moroni 10:34; see also Enos 1:27). Our own decision to stop climbing is the one thing we need fear. An eternity of chances awaits us. We cannot break the stairs; they are always inviting, continually reforming, and every failure finds forgiveness in the Stair Builder. The one fear is inactivity. We must never stop. We must never retreat. Life is our perpetual teacher.

All of life, I have learned, is the slow but steady acquiring of godliness. Some stairs are easier than others. I will struggle far beyond the grave to pass the step of patience—but only my own impatience will prevent it from coming at last. One of the saddest aspects of Christian history is the slow transformation of the definition of faith and how discipleship has become a measure of what we believe instead of how we treat others and what qualities of Christ we possess. Faith tends to be defined today as assenting to a particular set of statements about the nature of God and humankind, and their relationship to each other. Our own set of statements, the Articles of Faith, contains only one about how we act and treat others—Article 13. Some have tended to elevate faith in Christ as the highest single attribute of a disciple—one that is saving in itself. Whole religions are based on that. Yet as we have seen, Paul, who preached faith in Christ with such fervency, said, "And now abideth faith, hope, charity, these three; but the greatest of these is charity" (1 Corinthians 13:13). Charity trumps even faith—the Good Samaritan and Prodigal

Son above the Epistle to the Romans. We need not choose or become locked into battles of faith versus works—or your doctrine versus mine—as has so often happened between Christian groups. Our belief in Christ inspires us to follow Him, attempting to acquire all His attributes and perfections. It also acts as a catalyst to receive His necessary help with that task, and feeds the faith that each and every successful effort will find Him pleased and each and every failing effort will find Him merciful. I believe that is what the Atonement is all about. There is forgiving grace in Him and enabling grace also.

Peter, whose own journey to sanctification is detailed in the New Testament, taught that, beginning with faith in our Savior, we climb up the stairs, acquiring qualities of holiness and goodness until we reach charity—to live and love as Jesus did: "Giving all diligence, add to your faith virtue; and to virtue knowledge; and to knowledge temperance; and to temperance patience; and to patience godliness; and to godliness brotherly kindness; and to brotherly kindness charity. For if these things be in you, and abound, they make you that ye shall neither be barren nor unfruitful in the knowledge of our Lord Jesus Christ" (2 Peter 1:5–8). Notice that in this verse the qualities of a godly character come first and then we become fruitful in knowledge—which in turn perfects those qualities. This is what Abraham understood: to live like Christ is to know Him. If we claim to know Him without living as He lived, we deceive ourselves, in spite of all our doctrinal, faith-filled proclamations. To this journey, Peter attached the phrase "make your calling and election sure" (2 Peter 1:10).

There is space for only a few examples of the beauty and challenge of the stairs as I have come to know them, and my knowledge is limited; I'm still learning. Perhaps at the beginning we can no more than recognize the need for any particular stair in our own lives, but that need will grow into a desire to stand upon it—and move beyond it—out of love for God and the deep satisfaction of knowing we are becoming more and more like Him. Each of us will have our own story of how it felt to rise to the next stair, knowing that we had learned to be a tiny bit more like Jesus and His Father—and the humility that comes when thinking of how much further we might need to go. The following are a representative, but by no means exhaustive, list of examples and possible stairs, some of which are my favorites—or ones I would like most to ascend.

THE STAIR OF PERSUASION

I made many, many mistakes in leadership callings because I focused on loyalty and obedience from those over whom I presided. I was an earnest and sincere leader, from being a green district leader in France to serving in a stake presidency, from husband to father, but what I really needed was to look closely at the engravings on the stair I now call "persuasion." I found it one day while reading Doctrine and Covenants 121—the "many are called, but few are chosen" revelation (D&C 121:40).

I had read those verses a thousand times, but it finally sank in that *persuasion* was the first principle of righteous leadership. I had rarely heard that concept spoken of in my church experience. Furthermore, no "influence" could be "maintained" without it (D&C 121:41). The challenge was not the level of my children's or my district or ward or stake members' obedience, but rather my ability to persuade. If there were problems, in almost all cases they were mine to own. Commanding is easy, and moves responsibility from the leader to the follower—if someone doesn't follow my commands, it's not my fault.

It requires hardly anything to say, "We will do it *this* way because I want to or think it best." But to persuade, to reach unanimity, to see others not following behind, but walking together as equals takes more effort, takes counseling together about which particular course of action is the best and then obtaining the heartfelt agreement of one's spouse or children or stake members "by long-suffering, by gentleness and meekness, and by love unfeigned; by kindness, and pure knowledge" (D&C 121:41–42). Notice that all these words are qualities of soul. In their own way, they are all steps on the grand stairway to heaven. I love the stair of persuasion. I know I still fail from time to time to master it, but I take some comfort in seeing how difficult it is for others to master also. Yes, I recognize that this very attitude suggests I still have weights to clean out of my suitcase. Yet the principle is liberating and joy-instilling—much more satisfying than to command, expect loyalty, or anticipate obedience because of one's position.

The Apostle Paul gives us one of the best examples of persuasion in his Epistle to the Corinthians. The Saints in Corinth wrote to Paul justifying their eating of meat offered to idols—statues of the Greek and Roman gods. Undoubtedly these were times of national celebration and, as the Corinthians argued, "we know that an idol is nothing in the world" (1 Corinthians 8:4). "So what's the big deal if we eat a piece of meat that has been dedicated to Zeus or Athena? They don't exist and the meat is just a piece of meat." Nothing wrong with that thinking, is there? Paul patiently spends three chapters trying to *persuade* the Corinthians that their behavior is not consistent with the thinking of a Saint by using various arguments. (See 1 Corinthians 8–10.) His arguments are not important here—what I find compelling in this episode is that the issue had already been settled, as described in Acts 15, by a general council of the Church presided over by Peter and the other apostles. Letters had been written and sent to the various churches around the Mediterranean instructing the members to "abstain from meats offered to idols" (Acts 15:29). So why didn't Paul just tell the Corinthians, "The Brethren have said . . ."? He certainly could have, but he used persuasion instead and did not once mention the official Church position on this particular issue or cite his priesthood authority. I would love to master this stair.

THE STAIR OF NOT JUDGING NOR DESPISING

This episode brings to mind another stair of Christlike thinking and living that I learned from Paul and have tried to acquire. This stair is difficult, especially for Americans who are fixed on rights and "It's my life . . ."—and have trouble thinking otherwise. Some of the major themes in Paul's writing are about unity and charity. These he learned from the Savior himself. "I say unto you, be one; and if ye are not one ye are not mine," Jesus taught (D&C 38:27). In his Epistle to the Romans and then again in 1 Corinthians, Paul tackled a problem experienced by the early Saints. Some, probably Gentile converts, were eating food considered by the Jewish converts to be unclean. They were also not marking certain religious holidays the Jewish converts held sacred. There was no real necessity for Gentile converts to be good Jews before they could be good Christians; they had every right to eat what they wanted and do what they liked on certain days. But there was conflict between the two groups. Paul counseled: "Let not him that eateth *despise* him that eateth not; and let not him which eateth not *judge* him that eateth. . . . One man esteemeth one day above another: another esteemeth every day alike. Let every man be fully persuaded in his own mind" (Romans 14:3, 5; emphasis added).

I have sometimes called this concern "the despiser/judger dilemma"; I have found myself on both sides of this issue more times than I would like to acknowledge. In another verse, Paul writes, "But why dost thou judge thy brother? or why dost thou set at nought thy brother?" (Romans 14:10). I suppose we could also call it the judger/setter-at-nought problem. The non-eaters are judging the eaters, and the eaters couldn't care less what the non-eaters are thinking. Whenever I teach this concept, to make the issue relevant, I solicit despiser/judger conflicts from those I teach. People are always adding to my collection, often with a smile. It is always best to discuss these things with a healthy sense of humor. Some are occasionally a surprise to me, either that they are an issue or that some are so insistent on whether or not they are taboo. Here, in no particular order, are some of the things that Latter-day Saints tend to despise or judge each other regarding:

The Word of Wisdom Questions

Is caffeine okay so long as it's in a soda? Does chocolate contain caffeine? Is it okay to eat something cooked in wine? How much meat eating counts as "sparingly; [or] in times of winter, or cold, or famine"? (See D&C 89:12–13.)

The Gambling Questions

Are face cards evil? Is putting five dollars into the office pool for the NCAA basketball tournament gambling? Is playing bunko with your neighborhood friends?

The Dress and Grooming Questions

Can a man who has facial hair serve as a bishop? As an elders quorum president? As a temple ordinance worker? Can those who have been temple-endowed wear shorts? When and when not? Should a priesthood holder always wear a white shirt and tie to any Church meeting? Should women always wear hose to church?

Is it okay for a woman to pin back her garments so they don't peek out from a hemline or collar?

The Sabbath Questions

Is it okay to watch a football game on Sunday? To do homework? Can you crochet or knit in sacrament meeting? Is it okay to take over-the-counter medication when you're fasting? Have a drink from the drinking fountain at church?

The Cultural Questions

Have you made a choice to not "kill the little birds"?

How many children do you have? How many *should* you have? How large a house is enough? Does every member of your family need a separate bedroom?

What genres of music are acceptable to listen to on Sunday? During the rest of the week? Are there any genres of music that a good member of the LDS Church shouldn't ever listen to?

Can you be a good member of the LDS Church and a Democrat? A Libertarian? A Marxist? A Republican? Is it acceptable for a Latter-day Saint to characterize those with political views counter to their own as idiots or unrighteous?

Are certain words okay because they're "just cussing," and not "swearing"? Is it okay to substitute a nonsense word for a vulgarity or expletive? Is it "more honest" to swear like a sailor on shore leave?

That should be enough questions to get the point across. I would submit that if you didn't at least bristle at some of these, if you didn't find yourself somewhere on this list, then you're nearly to the top of the crystal stairs. Is one side the zealots, the religious fanatics? Is the other side the worldly group, the compromisers? Do we show contempt for those trying to live a standard, or censure those who see some (or all) of these standards as arbitrary?

Paul spoke to both sides. Addressing the judgers, he simply told them to stop it![1] "Who art thou that judgest another man's servant? to his own master he standeth or falleth" (Romans 14:4). Much of this is between us and our God. God has released us all from the need to judge. How relieving. We'll talk about mote-and-beam issues presently. What is so wonderful to me is Paul's counsel to the despiser, or the setter-at-nought part of the equation. He appeals to charity. Forget about rights or even if the behavior is correct or not: "If thy brother be grieved with thy meat, thou walkest not charitably if thou eatest" (JST, Romans 14:15). Then he lifts everyone to a higher level: "For the kingdom of God is not meat and drink; but righteousness, and peace, and joy in the Holy Ghost. . . . Let us therefore follow after the things which make for peace, and things wherewith one may edify another. . . . It is good neither to eat flesh, nor drink wine, nor any thing whereby thy brother stumbleth, or is offended, or is made weak. . . . Let every one of us please his neighbor for his good to edification" (Romans 14:17, 19, 21; 15:2). To the Corinthians, who were quite concerned about what they were allowed to do because they had "liberty" and "knowledge," Paul wrote: "Take heed lest by any means this liberty of yours become a stumbling-block. . . . If meat make my brother to offend, I will eat no flesh while the world standeth, lest I make my brother to offend" (1 Corinthians 8:9, 13). Paul was concerned that the example of the eaters might lead another, who had been brought up not eating, to do the same thing—but so doing would then "wound their . . . conscience" (1 Corinthians 8:12). To Paul's mind, it is never good to go against conscience, even if the conscience is overwrought and incorrect in its assessment. Time might ameliorate this.

If my daughter had five friends who all thought it was okay to see a particular movie, but she was concerned about some aspect of it, would it not be wonderful if, instead of badgering her or pressuring her or making fun of her or despising her for her ultra-strict standard, they simply said, "We'll go see one we all feel comfortable seeing." Don't worry about your rights, about what you're allowed to do, Paul is saying. It doesn't matter what knowledge you have; make your decision based on charity. If we knew that our cola drinking, our wearing of shorts, our putting five dollars in the office pool, our Sunday football watching, our blue-shirt-and-no-tie in elders quorum, our annual beard-growing contest for the deer hunt, and on and on, really was troublesome to others, we would stop—not because anything was wrong with those things and not because others might be judging us for doing them, but out of love and a desire for unity—and because they are such small things compared to the grand principles of the gospel. I have worn enough white shirts in my life to never want to buy another one as long as I live; my feelings toward ties are even more hostile. I truly believe ties are a vestige of medieval hypocrisy, but if I knew that someone in my ward was distressed with my wearing colored or pin-striped shirts on Sunday—whether their distress was caused by a standard they were living or a temptation to follow my "rebellious" example, or any other reason—I hope I would have the charity necessary to put on the white shirt. I want this stair and I want it badly.

A warning: the most dangerous thing we can do when reading Paul on this matter is to apply the instructions to the other guy and not to ourselves. It is not for the judger to say to the (in his eyes) less-circumspect member, "See, you need to stop hunting—and throw those shorts away, I can see your temple garments." He is to stop judging completely. Remember, God has released us all from the need to judge because we are so prone to get it wrong. He will do all the judging. It is also not for the despiser to say to the (in her eyes) overly-circumspect, "See, I can do what

I want, and I want to play bunko and wear flip-flops to church; quit being such a censoring zealot." She is to change where she can for the sake of unity and love. It is a difficult stair to stand on, but may be one of the highest marks of a mature disciple.

THE STAIR OF MOTES AND BEAMS

What if the weaknesses of others are real, and not just questionable or perceived or in a gray area? (I am aware that some of the earlier examples are not considered gray for many people.) I think there is a stair we could call the "mote-or-beam stair." I don't know why it is so pleasing to our minds to see the failings of others and somehow feel better about ourselves because of them, but it is human nature, the natural man, which is so hard to shake. I'm no different than the rest of you. Motes are easy to discover in our fellowmen (even if we have to look past our own beams to find them), and since everyone has them, we can spend a great deal of time focused on them. The temptation will always be there. Ah, sad humanity! Sad realization as well to know that we can always find faults if we look for them!

There are no motes or beams at the top of the stairs; their presence just slows our climbing. We would keep our eyes on He who climbs before us, not the soul that is next to us. Paul taught the Galatians, "Let every man prove his own work, and then shall he have rejoicing in himself alone, and not in another" (Galatians 6:4). He gave this counsel because the members were comparing their own best with their brother's or sister's worst. "If a man be overtaken in a fault, . . . restore such an one in the spirit of meekness. . . . Bear ye one another's burdens," he said (Galatians 6:1–2).

I think my favorite story about Joseph Smith deals with his own standing on this stair of motes and beams. He learned to turn inward, to ask "Lord is it I?" even when undergoing the intense and frequently unjust scrutiny of his fellowmen, both enemy and friend. Jesse Crosby tells this story:

"I went one day to the Prophet with a sister. She had a charge to make against one of the brethren for scandal. When her complaint had been heard the Prophet asked her if she was quite sure that what the brother had said of her was utterly untrue.

"She was quite sure that it was.

"He then told her to think no more about it, for it could not harm her. If untrue it could not live, but the truth will survive. Still she felt that she should have some redress.

"Then he offered her his method of dealing with such cases for himself. When an enemy had told a scandalous story about him, which had often been done, before he rendered judgment he paused and let his mind run back to the time and place and setting of the story to see if he had not by some unguarded word or act laid the block on which the story was built. If he found that he had done so, he said that in his heart he then forgave his enemy, and felt thankful that he had received warning of a weakness that he had not known he possessed.

"Then he said to the sister that he would have her to do the same: search her memory thoroughly and see if she had not herself unconsciously laid the foundation for the scandal that annoyed her.

"The sister thought deeply for a few moments and then confessed that she believed that she had.

"Then the Prophet told her that in her heart she could forgive that brother who had risked his own good name and her friendship to give her this clearer view of herself."[2]

Wouldn't we all love to mount that stair? Joseph was not looking for the motes in others' eyes, but searching for the beam in his own. That is one of the reasons he could see spiritual things so clearly. He was a seer—or see-er. He points the way in this story, and in order to view the timeless and everlasting, we must not let the dust spots—or timbers—of each others' failures block the eternal scenery. Remember, the man born blind washed first—and then he "came seeing."

There is a moving scene in Shakespeare's *Measure for Measure* that illustrates our point perfectly. As the title of the play indicates, the play's theme is concerned with judging and the Savior's declaration that how we assess others will be used as our own measure of judgment. Shakespeare explores that delicate tipping point between justice and mercy and the role of both. In the play, Isabella pleads for the life of her brother Claudio, whose lover, Juliet, carries his child, against the puritanical and justice-wielding Angelo: "If he had been as you and you as he, you would have slipped like him, but he, like you, would not have been so stern."[3]

When Angelo counters with his continued determination to condemn in the name of justice so that others will not sin, Isabella appeals to the Savior's own atoning mercy: "Why, all the souls that were were forfeit once; and He that might the vantage best have took found out the remedy. How would you be if He which is the top of judgement should but judge you as you are? O, think on that, and mercy then will breathe within your lips, like man new made."[4]

Mercy, forgiveness, redemption, and reconciliation were major themes in many of Shakespeare's plays, which is one of the reasons he was so great. He had the ability to be whoever he created and thus he sympathized with all humanity. No writer will be great who fails to cultivate that worldview—nor person, for that matter.

THE STAIR OF WRITING ON STONE

Juliet's and Claudio's sin and Isabella's plea draw my mind to a woman dragged before the Savior while He was teaching on the temple mount in Jerusalem, a very public place. This is a well-known story and I'm not sure I can add any insight to the beauty of the Savior's few simple words, but I will share what desire it has instilled in me separate from the extension of mercy.

When the woman taken in adultery was brought forward and her failing trumpeted before the world, the Savior's first response was to say nothing at all. We read, "Jesus stooped down, and with his finger wrote on the ground, as though he heard them not" (John 8:6). He wrote on the stone pavement of the temple mount with his finger. He did not rise to challenge them to cast the first stone, if they themselves had no sin—until they continued to push her immorality and demanded judgment from him. He answered them first with silence—a silence that loudly proclaimed, "I don't wish to hear of the sins and weaknesses of others, certainly not in so public and shaming a place and manner as you have done. I will stoop to write on the ground but I will not stoop to share in your seeming delight at this woman's fall. I will not write her act in my mind or in my heart."

That is how I would like to respond when the failings, weaknesses, sins, mistakes, behaviors, and offenses of others are offered to my ear for comment or assessment. And I'm talking about more than petty gossip or the public's fascination with the scandals of well-known people. There is—I wish it were not so—a tendency in us to find a certain pleasure in hearing about and dwelling on other's inadequacies. Granted, it is born of curiosity, but leads to an unhealthy satisfaction and at its worst, a smug pride. Because we are all human and aware of our own shortcomings, it unfortunately makes us feel a little better about ourselves to compare ours with others. Paul said that charity "thinketh no evil; rejoiceth not in iniquity" (1 Corinthians 13:5–6). Charity must of necessity have others as its object; when we hear of evil or iniquity in others, our response should not pass along that evil or iniquity. As did Jesus on this occasion, our charity should find no pleasure in the knowledge. Jesus did not want the details; He did not lean forward to hear. He shut them all out by simply stooping and writing on the stone. There it would leave no mark.

I have wanted to master this stair for a long time. When others' troubles or failings come to my attention, I want to write on the stone as though I hear them not.

I gave in to this temptation recently while with friends who opened a conversation by talking about the foolish behavior of an acquaintance. Our dialogue was not mean-spirited or even too judgmental and I was mostly silent, but I left the conversation feeling hollow. I should have changed the subject, but failed to do so. I had tasted that subtle flavor of delight in another's problem because it was not my own nor had I demonstrated similar foolish behavior in my own life. This happened just days before I was to depart for Australia. I had looked forward to visiting Uluru in the outback of Australia for many years; this dream was finally going to come true. But I was still feeling the unease of my failure to stand on a stair I have labored for (with scattered success) for at least as many years as I had wanted to visit this remarkable feature of creation. While hiking in Uluru I could not shake the self-disappointment at not being able to write on the stone. Subsequently the enjoyment of a once-in-a-lifetime experience was compromised. I stood on a sand dune looking at the high, red cliffs of the Australian outback and the Spirit said, "Why don't you leave this failure here. Never again let this weakness ruin another joyful experience." I don't know why I found such strength in that suggestion. But I left that weakness in the center of Australia, along with a few others. Every time the temptation arises, I visualize those things many thousands of miles away in the desert of Australia, and an ability to stand on the stair arrives with that thought.

THE STAIR OF INCLUSION

I learned much from another faith's ritual reading on Easter Sunday, and that leads me to another beautiful stair—that of openness, inclusion, and tolerance. We have all erected too many racial, religious, national, cultural, economic, and political barriers, not to mention the sad silliness of sports rivalries gone too far. These are all masks we wear that have no real enduring eternal value. We are all human beings, all offspring of God—that truth has enduring power. Paul wrote of Jesus, "He is our peace, who hath made both one, and hath broken down the middle wall of partition between us" (Ephesians 2:14). One of our roles is to break down walls. We do not want to be found building them up to seek solace behind them. Though doing so shows spiritual immaturity, almost all of us are still children in reaching for this stair.

I hate to admit that I grew up feeling somewhat sorry for everyone who was not a Californian or at least an American—and a bit suspicious of anyone from another faith. This was the "promised land," was it not? And by that I'm sure I thought that the West Coast of the United States was the most promised part of the promised land. I was more than a bit provincial. My journey outward began when I had the marvelous good fortune to marry a Canadian and found that she had absolutely no desire to be an American, let alone a Californian. She was completely content with her Alberta Canada heritage. I really was a bit stupid, and she kindly but firmly educated me. After nearly three decades of living in the States, she became a United States citizen, but it was more for legal and practical reasons. She died with the Maple Leaf securely embedded in her heart.

I remember one day coming home from the LDS Family History library, where I had been researching one of my early American lines. I had discovered that morning that one branch of my direct lineal descent had fought on the side of the British in the American Revolution out of Fort Niagara with the Iroquois tribe. My father was a member of the Sons of the American Revolution and also a Mayflower descendant. American history had also always been one of my own passions, so you can imagine how it hit me to learn I had Tories in my past. After the war, they were forced to leave New York and settled in Pickering, near Toronto, Ontario, Canada. I came home really down and told Laurie I had discovered a skeleton in the closet. Somewhat concerned, as she could see my distress, she asked me what I had found. "I have Tories in my ancestry," I replied. At this she stood up to her full 5' 3", bristled with indignation, and said: "You mean United Empire Loyalists? Some of the founders of Canada? I would give anything to have them in my ancestry. I will trade you my Virginia Planters for your Ontario Loyalists!" This was one of many such moments in my education. For years afterward we laughed about my lack of perspective.

God once showed Moses all the lands and peoples of the earth, then expanded that to include "worlds without number." Though they were innumerable to man, "all things are numbered unto me, for they are mine and I know them" (Moses 1:35). I should like to think that the sentiments of that scriptural phrase could apply to all of us—not in the same manner that they apply to God, for our minds are limited, but that all peoples, cultures, and nations could be simply, "mine," and that we could "know them." Paul told the citizens of Athens that God "hath made *of one blood* all nations of men for to dwell on all the face of the earth" (Acts 17:26; emphasis added). I have been blessed with the opportunity to travel a great deal in my latter years and have discovered that goodness, truth, and beauty—God's footprints—can be found everywhere. That opens up the heart, and I know my Californian heart needed opening, perhaps more than others. I used to think in terms of a universal apostasy which left the world in near total darkness. I have since learned that there has been much light to discover—in every age, among all peoples—so much that my soul and mind cannot hold it all. We have so much we can learn from each other. God has spread His truth over all the earth and we are allowed, encouraged even, to gather it and bring it into one edifying whole. Mou Tzu, a devout Buddhist Chinese sage, once commented on what we can learn from each other. Religions and cultures need not be ever in either/or, right/wrong confrontations. "Why should I reject the way of Yao, Shun, Confucius, and the Duke of Zhou [the traditional Chinese sages in Confucianism]? Gold and jade do not harm each other; crystal and amber do not cheapen each other."[5]

Erasmus of Rotterdam was an early humanist during the Renaissance and Reformation and was one of the great souls of history. He provided for us a summit of tolerance, openness, and inclusiveness to which we can climb. His words have come to us from various places and in different translations, but the sentiments cannot be doubted. "The whole world is my homeland," he said. "The entire world is my temple and a very fine one too." "I am a citizen of the world, my homeland is everywhere." "A certain person of importance at Zurich has more than once written to offer me the right of citizenship there; I wondered why he should do this, and replied that I preferred to be a citizen of the world, rather than of any one city."

I am in the Middle East a great deal and am often asked

about safety and other issues there, and what I think about the prophecies or hope for successful peace in that region. Usually the questioner is working under the assumption that, due to scriptural statements, there can really be no peace until the millennium. I like to show them a prophecy from Isaiah that I think about every time I go to this troubled region, but I think we can broaden its beautiful truth to other places in the world where division haunts the people. We tend to think in polar opposites. One side must be right and should have our allegiance. Yet I perceive our Father in Heaven may not see us in terms of such separation. To understand Isaiah's vision of the future, it is good to remember that when he recorded this scripture, Egypt and Assyria were enemies, with the tribes of Israel caught in the middle of broader regional conflicts—much as they are today. Isaiah wrote: "In that day shall there be a highway out of Egypt to Assyria, and the Assyrian shall come into Egypt, and the Egyptian into Assyria, and the Egyptians shall serve with the Assyrians. In that day shall Israel be the third with Egypt and with Assyria, *even a blessing in the midst of the land:* Whom the Lord of hosts shall bless, saying, Blessed be *Egypt my people*, and *Assyria the work of my hands*, and *Israel mine inheritance*" (Isaiah 19:23–25; emphasis added). There does not seem to be any preference with the Lord. "My people," "the work of my hands," and "mine inheritance" suggest an equality and breadth of love we would anticipate with our Father in Heaven.

THE STAIR OF THE BURNING BUSH

I believe one of the most beautiful images of God is that of the burning bush. Fire brings warmth, light, tempering, and purification, all of which our Father in Heaven can do for us. But in the case of the burning bush, the fire did not consume; it did no harm. So it is with God. However, what I would call attention to in relation to this stair is part of the conversation between God and Moses. Moses was concerned about the suffering and oppression of his people. Why had God done nothing to relieve their suffering? Can we not all relate somewhat to the situation in Exodus? I can't tell you how many times in my life I have pondered on human suffering and wondered why God let it happen or, even more often, why He seems to do nothing about it. If He is good (as He is) and all powerful (as He also is), why not alleviate the misery of so much of mankind? I recently was asked by a very young and very unhappy girl whose family was undergoing some traumatic blows, "If God loves me and wants us happy, why do these things happen?" There was such poignancy in the quiet, almost apologetic way she asked it.

At the burning bush, God told Moses, "I have surely *seen* the affliction of my people . . . and have *heard* their cry . . . I *know* their sorrows; and I am come down to *deliver* them . . . and *bring* them . . . unto a good land" (Exodus 3:7–8; emphasis added). I love the verbs in these verses. God sees, hears, knows, delivers, and will bring us into a good situation. I'm sure when Moses heard these words he was overjoyed that now, finally, something was going to be done to relieve the oppression and sadness of his people—and God himself was going to do it. He had "come down" for that very purpose. But a few verses later we learn how God generally comes down. "Come now therefore, and I will send thee . . . that thou mayest bring forth my people" (Exodus 3:10). Moses felt absolutely inadequate and tried to talk the Lord out of his own role in the deliverance, but the Lord knew the man and what he could accomplish. When Moses left the burning bush, it was as God's answer to tyranny and suffering. This is God's way. He generally uses those who see and hear and know as He does to do the delivering. I am too prone to expect Him to exercise His power and fix the problem while I cheer Him on and express gratitude for His mercy. Yet God seems to say to us, "You see the need. You know the problem. I will send you to fix it. You will be my answer." I collect what I call "burning bush" stories, tales of people who saw a need, saw suffering, and tried, often beyond imagination, to attend to it. I will give you but one example from this collection.

Charles Dickens was not only a great writer but a social reformer. It was suggested more than once that he could win a seat in Parliament, but he felt he could address the tragedies of the poor and marginalized of society better with his pen—and he was right. *A Christmas Carol* continues to be a force for calling our attention to the desperate emptiness of poverty. I can't think of a novel he wrote that did not address this problem. Dickens used to walk the streets of London for hours, often late at night. He frequented prisons and the poorest sections of the great city. He was particularly aware of the bleak lives of children and of young women who in desperation often turned to selling themselves in order to survive. He had gained the patronage of a Miss Coutts, a wealthy woman who supported whatever project Dickens suggested.

Together they formed what became an obsession for many years of his life—a home to take young women off the streets and move them into a new life. Urania Cottage was bought. It stood away from the city center. Dickens furnished it in a comfortable manner, chose matrons to work with the girls, then filled it with women from the streets. There was a garden in which the young women could grow flowers and vegetables. He called it simply "The Home," and that is what it felt like for these girls. They were treated with respect, often visited by Dickens, fed well, given their own space and bed, schooled, and taught useful trades. To return them to the streets of London would have invited a return to old ways, so passage was arranged to Canada, South Africa, or Australia, where they could begin a new life in the colonies. Their many descendants testify to Dickens's compassion. He could not save all the destitute of London, and he did not succeed with all he brought into the Home, but he heeded the call from the burning bush, and did what he could. He mastered this stair. As Claire Tomalin, a Dickens biographer, said: "He did what he did because he believed it was needed. If there was a providence in the fall of a sparrow, these girls were his sparrows, and he wanted to make them fly, not fall."[6]

President Thomas S. Monson tells a story from the journal of Joseph Millett which is another touching example of one who stood upon the stair of the burning bush. In Joseph Millett's own words: "One of my children came in, said that Brother Newton Hall's folks were out of bread. Had none that day. I put . . . our flour in sack to send up to Brother Hall's. Just then Brother Hall came in. Says I, 'Brother Hall, how are you out for flour.' 'Brother Millett, we have none.' 'Well, Brother Hall, there is some in that sack. I have divided and was going to send it to you. Your children told mine that you were out.' Brother Hall began to cry. Said he had tried others. Could not get any. Went to the cedars and prayed to the Lord and the Lord told him to go to Joseph Millett. 'Well, Brother Hall, you needn't bring this back if the Lord sent you for it. You don't owe me for it.' . . . You can't tell how good it made me feel to know that the Lord knew that there was such a person as Joseph Millett."[7] It is wonderful sometimes to be God's answer.

THE STAIR OF REFINEMENT

Thinking of Charles Dickens brings me to another stair I have come to value very much, especially in the latter years of my life. Maybe it is really several stairs, but I tend to link them in my thinking. It is the refinement/learning/time stair. Time itself is a gift and it has been good for me to occasionally ask myself how I am spending it. Am I learning what is worth knowing? Am I engaged in improving my thinking and my appreciation of noble things? Am I seeking the refined, cultured, or, in Paul's words, also enshrined in our Articles of Faith, am I thinking about "whatsoever things are true, whatsoever things are honest, whatsoever things are just, whatsoever things are pure, whatsoever things are lovely, whatsoever things are of good report; if there be any virtue, and if there be any praise" (Philippians 4:8; see also Articles of Faith 1:13).

Joseph Smith changed the verb in Paul's admonition from *think* to "we *seek* after these things" (Articles of Faith 1:13; emphasis added). *Seek* is even more active than *think*. This usually takes me into the realm of literature, theater, music, art, history, biography, architecture, science, and so many other fields of study and human endeavor. What am I trading my time in obtaining? Am I learning, and if so, in what field and at what rate?

I must admit I hated school as a boy. After kindergarten, it was all downhill until I reached college. Maybe mandatory learning with tests and grades will always be alien to me, but I don't have to do that anymore. There comes a time in our lives when we can learn for the sheer joy of expanding our minds and refining our spirits. I believe the Lord is pleased when learning becomes a passion, especially if it is balanced with compassionate action. I suspect that an honest assessment might reveal to us all that we spend a great deal of time in being entertained—and that much of it does not expand, enlighten, or refine. I recently read an advertisement for a television provider which simply said: "Because in the end it's the entertainment that matters." Could the problem have been stated any better? There are a great many more things that matter and on a much higher level than our entertainment.

Now, we don't want to take ourselves too seriously; laughter can be a healthy medicine. I enjoy a Saturday football game as well as anyone, but I usually don't exit thinking, "Wow, that really changed me! What the world needs is more of this!" For the participants, who trained their bodies with diligence, habit, and determination, the time can certainly be well-used and, for the rest of us, we need to rest our brains from time to time, but perhaps we put too high a premium on entertainment for its own sake. Since the advance of electronic media, concerns have only intensified as video games and Internet usage engulf massive amounts of time. Their rapidly changing images and stimulation give us an attention deficit when more, not less, thought is required. It might be a truism of life that if we are not receiving higher-quality aesthetic fulfillment, we will naturally descend to sensual satisfaction—and the entertainment industry knows a great deal about that. There seems to be something inside that wants artistic refinement, but if that is not supplied, the baser instincts step into its place. It appears there is no neutral ground in this area. I described earlier Dickens's "Home" for destitute girls; one of his considerations was educating their minds with good literature. In a letter to Miss Coutts, whose money supported the Home, he wrote: "If their imaginations are not filled with good things, they will choke them, for themselves, with bad ones."[8]

I recall sitting in an English class in high school early in the school year. The teacher, whom I idolized—she was young and very pretty and I think all of us boys were a little in love with her—asked us what authors we were reading. When I told her one of my own favorites, she was not impressed and tried to get me to see there were better ways of engaging my brain. In defense, I pushed back a little, which led her to say—and I will never forget her words—"Mr. Wilcox, the reason you like that author is that the only taste you have is in your mouth." That stung a bit. She said it with a touch of humor and a slight smile, but I could tell she was serious and somewhat disappointed in me, having expected higher things. She then read to us some of the beautiful words and ideas from the world's great literature and I saw immediately she was right. There was a world of difference; I promised myself on that day that I would learn to have taste somewhere other than just in my mouth. I'm not sure how well I have succeeded, but I have earnestly tried.

Since the crystal stairs are, in so many ways, a climb into greater and higher levels of morality and goodness, the constant refining of the soul—how we nourish our hearts and minds—will direct in many ways our climb. We may ignore what are often called "the humanities" to the detriment of both our moral and religious growth. Charles Darwin, who had one of the most curious minds of the nineteenth century, early in his life enjoyed music and read Shakespeare. These pursuits faded as he focused almost exclusively on science. At the end of his life, he made an interesting comment: "If I had to live my life over again, I would have made a rule to read some poetry and listen to some music at least once every week; for perhaps the parts of my brain now atrophied would thus have been kept active through use. The loss of these tastes is a loss of happiness, and may possibly be injurious to the intellect, and more probably to the moral character, by enfeebling the emotional part of our nature."[9]

Time spent in service and compassion is climbing. Time spent in family love and sharing is climbing. Time spent in learning is climbing. Time spent in refining cultural pursuits is climbing. I'm not sure—other than its recuperative value in periodically relaxing the mind—that time spent in entertainment equals climbing. At its worst, it prevents or reverses it. Perhaps our nation—our world—has elevated it to too high a position. If refinement and culture is not a stair in and of itself, the good energy and motivation it gives will aid us on our climb. The Preacher of Ecclesiastes wrote, "A wise man's heart discerneth both time and judgment. Because to every purpose there is time and judgment" (Ecclesiastes 8:5–6). This follows with a common theme in Ecclesiastes: the uncertain future. Time and judgment are an insightful linkage. We are invited to use judgment in the time we are all given. How will we spend those precious hours and days and months and years? Paul used a wonderful word when speaking about time. "Redeeming the time," was his counsel (Ephesians 5:16). *Redeeming* adds a semi-sanctity to the use of our time. Emma Smith (and, through her, all women, for this section ends with "this is my voice unto all" [D&C 25:16]) was encouraged with the words, "thy time shall be given . . . to learning much" (D&C 25:8). In one of the key sections of the Doctrine and Covenants, the Lord tells His flock to "cease to be idle" (D&C 88:124). In another section He counseled, "Thou shalt not idle away thy time" (D&C 60:13). The word *idle* usually means doing nothing and is often associated with physical tasks—or avoiding physical tasks. However, perhaps the Lord is asking the question, "When you don't have anything to do, what *do* you do?" That question can reveal something of our interior landscape, of our priorities. I have found that attempting to ascend the stair of refinement, using time for worthwhile learning and improvement, offers rewards well beyond the effort required to climb it. And I suppose this is true of each and every step in the crystal stairs.

THE STAIR OF CONTENTMENT

We live in a bustling culture which values the Protestant work ethic—diligence, frugality, labor, accomplishment, ambition, achievement, and so forth. The Reformation's elevation of work was one of its best gifts. It gave dignity to the common laborer and challenged the privileged idleness of the upper classes. It's certainly no coincidence that the symbol of the state of Utah is the beehive and "Industry" its motto.

One of the reasons we might fall short in our attempts to master the stair of refinement is our occupation with what has become so much a part of Western civilization's activity. For many, business represents the real world. I would not challenge the values and ethic that has produced so much good in the world, but as with anything, there can be a down side. In our ambition-driven world, we may lose perspective. I tend to be achievement oriented, somewhat restless and activity obsessed, and have had to learn something about the stair of contentment—contentment with myself as well as my surroundings. Contentment brings an internal peace. This stair represents more than a count-my-blessings satisfaction with life, but is an acceptance of life. We probably all fight life a bit too much instead of flowing with it. Eastern peoples and religions are much better at this. It is difficult to see Jesus in the typical Western work ethic. The accumulations and achievements of success had no attraction for Him; He was content with very little. Yet I doubt there was a happier man on earth in spite of the great burden of sorrow He carried for the world.

Paul wrote to Timothy that he had "learned, in whatsoever state I am, therewith to be content." He had learned this from being "instructed" by the ever-changing details of life (Philippians 4:11–12). This instruction came from both times of abundance and times of want, success and failure, up and down. Learning was the key thing. In another epistle, he suggested that "godliness with contentment is great gain. For we brought nothing into this world, and it is certain we can carry nothing out. And having food and raiment let us be therewith content" (1 Timothy 6:6–8). The key to Paul's attitude is its linking godliness to contentment. He is moving up the eternal, crystal stairs and that is much more satisfying than moving up the ladder of success.

One of my sweetest memories of traveling in the world occurred in Myanmar, at Bagan, a broad plain covered with temples and stupas built in honor of the Buddha. There are thousands of these memorials of every size. In this setting of splendor and crumbling ruins, a small boy approached me with a handful of homemade postcards consisting of drawings of the landscape he had colored with crayons. "One dollar," he said and held out his masterpieces. I have seen children of every description selling souvenirs in many countries, but there was something about the handmade cards that caught me a bit off guard emotionally. I pulled out a dollar and the exchange was made, but his reaction was exceptional. He leaped in the air and began to dance, crying with delight, then turned and ran down the road, dust bursting in little clouds from his feet, waving the dollar back and forth in triumph. He took it to his father and presented it to him proudly. About ten minutes later, I saw him in the shade of a tree wearing a look of utter satisfaction and contentedly drinking a soda pop. Oh, to find that level of contentment in such simple accomplishments and pleasures!

The stair of contentment does not apply just to material things or achievements or success, but also to whatever life deals you. There is an Islamic Sufi story told about a king who could never come to terms with life and was tossed between satisfaction and despair. How could he come to peace? He asked a wise man in his kingdom who seemed serene and tranquil in all conditions to give him the secret of a life of contentment and balance. He was willing to pay a great price for the knowledge, but the man of wisdom declined the offer of wealth. He returned later with a beautiful box which he gave to the king with the assurance that the key to a contented life lay within. Inside was a ring with words engraved on it; the king was to wear the ring always and read the words daily. He read four words and their profound simplicity changed his life. "This too will pass." Did the words have more meaning when things were not going well? Or were they equally applicable when all was right? Either way, life is change. The problems will depart, that is good—and yet we learn so much from them. The delights will also depart—so enjoy them instead of hoping, sometimes desperately, that nothing will upset the soft rhythms of one's life.

Too often we wait for some change before we believe we can enjoy life. I am as guilty of this as anyone. The key is to appreciate, to value and relish what we are doing, to live at least as much in the now as we do in the future, or, even more futile, the past. Jiddu Krishnamurti, a contemporary Indian spiritual teacher, was speaking in California when he paused in the middle of his discussion and told his audience he would give them the secret of his own life. It was a spontaneous gesture and anticipation filled the room. What would this wise man who had thought long and hard about life offer? "You see," he said, "I don't mind what happens." Just five simple words! Or, in three words of one of the Beatles's most famous songs, "Let it be."[10] This is not always easy (or even possible), but within this philosophy we will find a road to contentment. This does not mean we practice resignation, rather acceptance, and there is a world of difference between the two. One leans to the negative, the other to the positive side of our thinking.

Isaiah invited his people to consider the night sky: "Lift up your eyes on high, and behold who hath created these things, that bringeth out their host by number: he calleth them all by names by the greatness of his might, for that he is strong in power; not one faileth" (Isaiah 40:26). Isaiah then gave the reason for his desire that we look into the galaxy. The God who can create, know, and hold all these worlds in their orbits will bless those that "wait upon" Him. "The Lord shall renew their strength; they shall mount up with wings as eagles; they shall run, and not be weary; and they shall walk, and not faint" (Isaiah 40:31). I have tried to follow Isaiah's advice, though I sometimes forget and need to be reminded.

Occasionally we ought to go outside, away from the lights of the city, and look into the night sky. All those stars—all that space! There is a serene awe that accompanies the vast scene before us. Timelessness flows through those galactic swirls. Though space is infinite, we do feel God is there. It helps us become somewhat detached from worldly cares. Problems seem smaller because they are. In comparison to the dance of the universe, they are truly fleeting and inconsequential. I don't know if this works for everyone, but it calms me down, especially when I consider that I am a part of that grand creation. It will endure and so will I. We are eternal things. The God who created that majesty also created me. In that landscape, being and becoming seem more compatible than doing, or achieving, or having—and contentment arises.

THE STAIR OF "NOTWITHSTANDING" AND "NEVERTHELESS"

Some of the most instructive lessons arising from Jesus' life are contained in the less-noticed stories or brief words He spoke or drew from the minds of His disciples. Ever since I was little and fished, I loved the story of Peter drawing a fish from the Sea of Galilee and finding a coin in its mouth. The story begins with a question that Jesus' critics asked Peter. "They that received tribute money came to Peter, and said, Doth not your master pay tribute? He saith, Yes." Peter was defending his Master from criticism. Tribute money was required to support the temple in Jerusalem. Since this was His Father's house—indeed His own house—though Peter attested otherwise, payment was not necessary for Jesus. As Peter entered the house, Jesus stopped him with a question. "What thinkest thou, Simon? of whom do the kings of the earth take custom or tribute? of their own children, or of strangers? Peter saith unto him, Of strangers. Jesus saith unto him, *Then are the children free*" (Matthew 17:24–26; emphasis added). In essence, Jesus told Peter, "This is something I don't need to do." Most of us, presented with this type of situation, would stand on our rights. If I don't need to do it, I don't need to do it. Or, if I am entitled to it, I am entitled to it. Especially in America, we are rights-oriented and individualistic—often without regard to others' perceptions. We surely say, and say quite strongly, "Then are the children free." What Jesus says next about the tribute money portrays such a quality of personality and character that I admire and wish to obtain in my own approach to human relations: "*Notwithstanding*, lest we should offend them, go thou to the sea, and cast an hook" (Matthew 17:27; emphasis added). The rest of the story continues with Peter catching a fish and finding a coin in its mouth, but for me, the miracle is not what really matters.

The key word that holds the great truth of this moment is *notwithstanding*. The Savior chose not to give offense, or stand on His rights, or invite contention, or protect His space, or defy convention, or create tension. He simply decided to not give offense.

There are many times in my own life when I have tried to say "notwithstanding" to a situation. Of course, I fail continually, but when we *can* avoid offense, as much as it is in our power, we should do so. There were times when Jesus acted differently because a principle needed emphasis, such as healing on the Sabbath. When I read the New Testament, I get the impression that He deliberately chose the Sabbath day to heal knowing the response He would get from His detractors. When the occasion warranted, He was not afraid to break the Pharisees' rules, but otherwise, He favored the "notwithstanding" approach. When we respond to the more negative qualities of our soul and actually take delight in correcting someone else, careless of the offense we might be giving, even relishing the moment, it is especially sad. Have we, perhaps, all been on the receiving and giving end of painful moments, when a cannon of criticism was leveled but a peashooter of corrective counsel would have been sufficient?

We see a similar moment in Jesus' life when He was rejected by the Samaritans because He was going to worship in Jerusalem. James and John, insulted by the rejection, are ready to call down fire from heaven, but Jesus defused the situation. We read the beautifully simple words, "And they went to another village" (Luke 9:56). There are certainly times when we need to, peacefully and without resentment (for I sense none in the Savior), go to another village, choosing neither to take nor give offense. We see this need in society at large, but also in our own personal relationships and family interactions. Many of my regrets center on my inability in the moment to say "notwithstanding" or to be able to walk away and go to another village to avoid a confrontation. I married a go-to-another-village woman and watched her spread calm over a potentially volatile situation more times than I can count. In many instances of our lives we must say, as Jesus did on the cross, "They know not what they do," and walk away (Luke 23:34).

Another word I deeply appreciate for the stair-climbing attitude it portrays comes from Peter's positive reaction to a command Jesus gave him. This took place on the day Jesus called Peter to follow him. Jesus taught the multitude from Peter's boat just off the shore so he would not be pressed by the crowds. When finished "he said unto Simon, Launch out into the deep, and let down your nets for a draught. And Simon answering said unto him, Master, we have toiled all the night, and have taken nothing." Who is the fisherman here and who the carpenter? Did not Peter know fishing better? Yet he followed up his mild opposition with the words, "nevertheless at thy word I will let down the net" (Luke 5:4–5). A great multitude of fish is then caught, but again, it is not the miracle of caught fishes that impresses me so much as that single word—"nevertheless."

We can often find ample reason why a certain command, counsel, or suggestion from the Lord—or His messengers—is not needful because of circumstances or our perceived expertise. But the wise say with Peter, "nevertheless," then obey or follow without needing convincing arguments or feeling that you are the exception. The scriptures are filled with nevertheless statements, offered by great men and women who did not always have a full understanding, but they responded with faith and anticipated confirmation. Here are a few:

- "I know not, save the Lord commanded me" (Moses 5:6).
- "Behold the handmaid of the Lord; be it unto me according to thy word" (Luke 1:38).
- "I will go and do the things which the Lord hath commanded. . . . And I was led by the Spirit, not knowing beforehand the things which I should do" (1 Nephi 3:7; 4:6).
- "Speak; for thy servant heareth" (1 Samuel 3:10).

Then there is the Savior's own plea to His Father to remove the cup, followed by the most significant "nevertheless" in human history. "O my Father, if it be possible, let this cup pass from me: nevertheless not as I will, but as thou wilt" (Matthew 26:39).

Let there be more notwithstandings, and going to other villages, and neverthelesses in our lives. To live thus is to master one of the lovely stairs in our ascent into being and becoming. They are the mark of spiritual maturity and awareness. They carry with them the assurance that we are pleasing to the Stair Builder, for He set the great example of these Himself.

CHAPTER SIX

THE ASCENT CONTINUES

His heart swelled wide
As eternity . . .
And all eternity shook.

—MOSES 7:41

There is an inner church which awaits at the very center of all religions, all faiths, certainly our own, that knows no theological or doctrinal borders. Belonging to this sanctified body of believers is my highest aspiration. I have no defining, encompassing name for it. I give it various titles: The Church of the Compassionate; of the Good-Hearted; of the Lovingly Humble and Merciful. I sense membership here is most critical, and so we continue our ascent with stairs I perceive invite us into the very core of religion, indeed, of God's heart.

THE STAIR OF MERCY

Conquering related stairs leads naturally to surmounting that of mercy—one of God's most endearing qualities. It is the very essence of the Atonement. I received great help in understanding this stair from the Russian and the Greek Orthodox churches. In Orthodoxy, Easter is the highest celebratory holy day. In Western Christianity, we value the Nativity, so Christmas occupies the place of honor. Each Easter morning, the faithful gather within their churches and listen to a sermon delivered more than a millennia and a half ago by John Chrysostom, who lived in the fifth century c.e. All stand in respect while it is being delivered.

The Easter Sermon contains an invitation derived from the Savior's parable of the laborers in the vineyard. For the Orthodox, this is a key teaching of the Savior. I have heard discussions and have read commentaries on this parable which try, sometimes painfully so, to reconcile the idea of justice and fairness with the lord of the vineyard's kindness in paying the one-hour laborers the same wage as the twelve-hour ones. We occasionally have trouble with this parable because we anticipate fairness. Justice is high on our list of expected qualities. And I suspect that we usually see ourselves as the twelve-hour laborers. We often call attention to the idea that if the one-hour laborers had been called earlier, they would have responded. That may be a legitimate point, but why make it at all? With our justice/fairness hat on, it can be so difficult to just let God be merciful and kind. Does He not say, "Friend, I do thee no wrong: . . . Is it not lawful for me to do what I will with mine own? Is thine eye evil, because I am good?" (Matthew 20:13, 15). What I sense the Savior is saying here is, "Friend, please don't turn my positive mercy to negative injustice. Let me be merciful and kind and good."

One of my daughters felt that I had been too easy on her

younger brother and we had a discussion about fairness and consistent justice among siblings. I recall asking her, "Do you want a just father or a merciful one?" I will never forget her answer. It was offered with a touch of humor, but was very human in its sentiments. "I want you to be just for Ben and merciful for me!" We laughed and the discussion ended.

Let us listen to the sermon delivered each Easter for centuries in those beautiful Greek and Russian Orthodox churches. When I first heard it, something changed in my heart. I had an epiphany of sorts and wanted to be as merciful as the call echoing through the ages because I comprehended something in the nature of God and Christ I had not realized as deeply before. It seemed as if the whole world was being invited to partake of God's compassion. Jesus said, "I am . . . the Rock of Heaven, which is broad as eternity" (Moses 7:53). That Rock is the rock of His compassion, His forgiveness, and His mercy—there is no end to it. In John Chrysostom's sermon, for whatever reason, I saw the etchings on the stair of mercy and wanted to follow the Stair Builder onto that step and beyond.

Is there anyone who is a devout lover of God?
Let them enjoy this beautiful bright festival!
Is there anyone who are grateful servants?
Let them rejoice and enter into the joy of their Lord!
Are there any weary with fasting?
Let them now receive their wages!
If any have toiled from the first hour,
let them receive their due reward;
If any have come after the third hour,
let him with gratitude join in the Feast!
And he that arrived after the sixth hour,
let him not doubt; for he too shall sustain no loss.
And if any delayed until the ninth hour,

let him not hesitate; but let him come too.
And he who arrived only at the eleventh hour,
let him not be afraid by reason of his delay.
For the Lord is gracious and receives the last even as the first.
He gives rest to him that comes at the eleventh hour,
as well as to him that toiled from the first.
To this one He gives, and upon another He bestows.
He accepts the works as He greets the endeavor.
The deed He honors and the intention He commends.
Let us all enter into the joy of the Lord!
First and last alike receive your reward;
rich and poor, rejoice together! . . .
Rejoice today for the Table is richly laden!
Feast royally on it, the calf is a fatted one.
Let no one go away hungry. Partake, all, of the cup of faith.
Enjoy all the riches of His goodness! . . .
Let no one mourn that he has fallen again and again;
for forgiveness has risen from the grave.[1]

Our Savior and His Father are inviting Gods. Surely justice is important and we shall stand on that stair one day and comprehend what it really is. But I think they favor mercy and kindness and elevate them to a higher rung on the ladder of salvation. I recall a moment of mercy I experienced one year while visiting the Sea of Galilee. We had been on the Sea that evening recounting the story of the Savior walking on the water and Peter's attempt to follow his Master even in this. On the darkness of the lake, you can almost visualize the figure of the Savior coming across the waves to his beloved disciples in their distress.

Early the next morning, in that period of waking sleep, of calm restlessness when we neither slumber nor rise but the mind is open and the memory stilled, I too was on the Sea, tossed by the storm and filled with terror. I could see my wife standing on the shore calling to me, but in spite of all my labors to swim to her, I was being carried farther and farther away. I had been caught in the riptides off the coast of California as a young man and knew well that desperate feeling when you swim with all your might and yet the shore continues to recede in the distance and you believe—you are almost certain—that you are going to drown. This was how I felt. I had no more strength to swim. The thought of leaving my wife was so devastating I gave up in despair and let the wind and waves take me. Then Jesus came. I could not see His face, only His feet standing on the water and His outstretched hand. I took it and He lifted me up as He had Peter and walked with me back to the shore. What was so beautiful about this experience was not my imagination placing me in a Bible story. We all do that, and it gives the Holy Spirit the opportunity to teach us personal truths, but I am touched by the fact that I had not even called upon Him for help. I did not cry out as did Peter, "Lord, save me" (Matthew 14:30). I had not thought of Him at all! I was only conscious that I was going to drown. Yet He came. That was a lesson in my life! Perhaps there is a connection to Matthew's story in this idea for I do not think the disciples were expecting the Savior to walk on the waves to their rescue. They were afraid and thought He was a spirit. He came without them calling, just as He did for me and just as He will for us all.

In our hymns, we sing that He "reaches my reaching."[2] This is true, beyond question, but He also reaches our un-reaching. And *that* is mercy indeed. The Psalmist wrote, "For as the heaven is high above the earth, so great is his mercy toward them that fear him. . . . Like as a father pitieth his children, so the Lord pitieth them that fear him" (Psalm 103:11, 13). I suppose we could add to the psalm, "and even to those that fear him not." Jesus taught, "For if ye love them which love you, what thank have ye?

. . . Love ye your enemies, and do good . . . and ye shall be the children of the Highest: for he is kind unto the unthankful and to the evil. Be ye therefore merciful, as your Father also is merciful" (Luke 6:32, 35–36). Can we not learn to do likewise with each other and stand upon that stair?

THE STAIR OF HUMILITY

The next stair is a particularly necessary one, but also a very difficult one to climb. Benjamin Franklin, examining his life and finding himself wanting in several areas, organized a program to incorporate those qualities he wanted to possess. These included thirteen virtues which he wanted to make habits through constant effort and concentration. He made a little book, devoting a page to each of the virtues. All of his choices could be considered a step on the climb upward. Here is his list—temperance, silence, order, resolution, frugality, industry, sincerity, justice, moderation, cleanliness, tranquility, chastity, and, last of all, humility. He originally had only twelve listed, but it was pointed out to him that he had a tendency toward pride, so he added humility as the thirteenth. To this last quality, Franklin simply wrote, "Imitate Jesus and Socrates." Franklin found his greatest challenge with humility.

That is a stair I too would dearly love to stand upon! How relieving it would be to step out of a skin that constantly needs to, for its own advantage, compare itself to others—for that is what pride does. Reflecting on what he was learning, Franklin later wrote, "I was surpris'd to find myself so much fuller of faults than I had imagined; but I had the satisfaction of seeing them diminish."[3] Yet humility eluded him. "In reality," he said, "there is perhaps no one of our natural passions so hard to subdue as *Pride*; disguise it, struggle with it, beat it down, stifle it, mortify it as much as one pleases, it is still alive, and will every now and then peep out and show itself; you will see it perhaps often in this history. For even if I could conceive that I had completely overcome it, I should probably be *proud* of my *humility*."[4] Franklin's conclusion is not one any of us would argue with, and from time to time the Lord helps us gain this essential quality by reminding us of our limitations.

Let me share one. I mentioned earlier how kind my doctoral chairman was with me. The day finally came when I defended my dissertation. It centered on the philosophy and writings of C. S. Lewis. I was confident, as my chairman told me I could be. When all the defending was over, the committee asked me one final question: "So, Mr. Wilcox, what has all this taught you?" It sounded innocent enough. How could I get that one wrong? But it caught me off guard.

I sensed something deeper in the question; the pressure was not coming so much from the five people in the room, but from another source. It seemed to me that in those few seconds I considered an answer, I was to assess not just the three years of PhD studies, but everything from kindergarten until that moment, a span of over thirty years. What had it all taught me? I believe the Lord was listening in. I suspect He might have inspired the question. Then, knowing I would get it wrong, the Spirit answered it for me. There are times when the Spirit simply takes over for us and we hear ourselves saying things we have never thought before. I could almost hear the words: "You will not get this right, but you need to know what your education has taught you, so I am going to answer it for you. Listen carefully to your own words; they are coming from me." I heard myself answer: "I have learned that I am an ignorant man, and that I have always been an ignorant man, and that I will always be an ignorant man. I have spent years of my life studying deeply the writings of one man, C. S. Lewis, and to be honest with you, I really don't know him very well. In light of all the knowledge that exists in so many fields of study, how much do any of us know? We are all ignorant men."

I guess they liked the response because they awarded me the degree. I was saved in those few moments from one danger, at least, in my life—the pride of learned men. I have been around universities for almost forty years and I know something of the pride they can create. The Book of Mormon warned, "O the vainness, and the frailties, and the foolishness of men! When they are learned they think they are wise" (2 Nephi 9:28). That answer also saved me from the fear of learned men when, either in the spoken or in the written word, I find them critical of or challenging my beliefs. I always try to listen and assess, because we can grow from contact with learned people, but in my heart I know they are just as ignorant as I am. I think it was worth all the years of my education, including the horror of junior high school (which I am convinced was invented by Lucifer), to come to that conclusion.

That answer created humility in me, at least in that one area, and it has I believe lasted. Years after my defense, it was gratifying for me to read the thoughts of Galileo, a man of broad curiosity, one of the great theorists in the history of the world, a brilliant man: "There is not a single effect in nature, not even the least that exists, such that the most ingenious theorists can ever arrive at a complete understanding of it. The vain presumption of understanding everything can have no other basis than [that of] never having understood anything. For anyone who had experienced just once the perfect understanding of one single thing, and had truly tasted how knowledge is attained, would recognize that of the infinity of other truths he understands nothing."[5] There was also a secondary blessing from this experience. It generated a deeper desire in me to learn in multiple areas. Learning can become a delightful obsession.

Humility is a virtue that must be nourished in many areas of life, for even if we have achieved it in one field it may be deficient in another and therefore this step on the grand stairway will be a lifelong pursuit. We will ultimately need to stand on the highest step of all, that of charity (or divine, selfless love), and humility may be the step just beneath, the one that lifts us up to that last grand prism. Mormon taught, "None is acceptable before God, save the meek and lowly of heart; and if a man be meek and lowly of heart . . . he must needs have charity" (Moroni 7:44). I recall another moment in my life when it was pointed out to me by the Spirit that I was lacking humility in my own assessment of my teaching. This came very early in my career and I have been extremely grateful that it did. It was a saving moment once again, though it happened earlier in my life.

I taught in Tempe, Arizona, during the first three years of my career, from when I was twenty-three to twenty-six. I was young and had a lot to learn. I loved teaching and had wonderful moments with those students. I became dear friends with many of them. I still remember them with such fondness. If you are successful with high school students, it is simply glorious. If you fail, they will make you wish you were dead. Fortunately, because of their good nature and, to be fair, a lot of hard work by myself, those three years were some of the best in my teaching career.

I was transferred at the end of the semester; the last official contact I would have with them was seminary graduation. I was moving to Canada and the likelihood of seeing many of them again would be remote. Because I was leaving, the topic of many of their speeches and testimonies during graduation centered on what a great teacher I had been, how much I had changed their lives, and how much they would miss me. The whole evening turned into a "thank-you-Brother-Wilcox-you're-wonderful" meeting. The trouble with hearing this kind of outward and gracious praise is that I might be tempted to believe it. I was not only tempted; I gave in. I might have looked up to heaven and thought, *Aren't you glad I'm on your side!* So the Lord had an inventory with me that evening. I've never had any experience quite like it again in my life. I could almost see Him enter the back of the chapel, walk down the aisle, and take the empty seat next to me as I sat on the stand. Then the questions began. They were gentle and filled with kindness, with just a touch of humor. He had not come to condemn, but to instruct and save me from myself, as He so often does.

"Whose children are these young men and women?" He began.

"They are your children, Lord," I answered.

"Whose church is this?"

"It is thy church."

"Who inspired this seminary program?"

"It came from thee, Lord."

"And whose scriptures are you teaching?"

"They are thy scriptures."

"If you can teach well, who gave you that gift of the Spirit?"

"It is thy gift."

"If there was a healing, inviting Spirit in the classroom, whose Spirit was it?"

"It was thy Spirit."

"If a life was changed because of what happened in the classroom, who really changed that life?"

"You changed their lives, Lord."

"Though they don't know it yet, because they are only beginning to mature spiritually, who were they really thanking at the pulpit this evening?"

There is only so much humility one can take. So I offered my last defense before being delightfully released into the humility God wished me to carry through my career in teaching, speaking, and also in writing—a lesson about this particular stair He didn't want me ever to forget.

"Don't I get a little credit?" I asked.

"No," He answered. "There is no credit, but you may thank me for the privilege of teaching my scriptures to my children with my Spirit in my seminary program."

So I thanked Him, and there was joy in that moment of adoration. When I was through, He said: "And I thank you for all you've done for my children!"

That was gracious and only served to deepen the humility and the love I felt for Him. It was a gentle chastisement, but not even perceived as one. I felt Him rise from the seat next to me and, once again, could almost visibly watch Him walk back down the aisle and exit the chapel. I have never changed a life in the many years of teaching, and speaking, and writing I have done. But I have been able to watch the Lord work wonderful transformations and have thanked Him for allowing me to witness them. As long as I feel this way, I rarely fail to receive His gracious, "And I thank you." It is one of the joys that come as we climb, for all the glory and gladness is not reserved for the top of the stairs.

THE STAIR OF THE EYES OF JESUS

The Stair of the Eyes of Jesus may not be the best name for this stair, but it is how I think of it. I had taught the life of the Savior for many years before the Spirit one day directed me to "see with the eyes of Jesus." This initiated a search. I went through all the stories I knew of Christ during His mortal mission, asking myself the questions: "How is He seeing others? If I were looking through His eyes, what would I see? What would I feel? What would I do?" I paid special attention when I found the words *looked*, *saw*, *beheld*, and so forth, when those words described Jesus. This proved to be one of the most fruitful searches I have ever conducted in the scriptures. Stories I had loved and that I thought I knew pretty well opened up to new dimensions. I will share only a few to illustrate this stair and will start with the two that, without question, are the closest to my heart.

Zacchaeus, the "little of stature" publican, condemned and despised by his fellow citizens of Jericho, wanted to see Jesus as he was passing through the town. Because the press of people was so great and no one would make room for him he climbed "into a sycamore tree to see him: for he was to pass that way." Can you see in your own imagination this little man sitting alone in the branches, unwelcomed and shunned? We then read the beautiful words, "And when Jesus came to the place, *he looked up, and saw him*" (Luke 19:4–5; emphasis added). How many people within the compass of our reach sit alone in the sycamore tree, abandoned by the "press" of other people? The Spirit has taught me to pray, "Father in Heaven, grant me the eyes of Jesus that I may look up and see those in the sycamore tree."

A few chapters earlier in Luke, Jesus told what I believe is the greatest story in human literature—that of the Prodigal Son. It overwhelms me every time I read it. And I would guess you all know the moment in the parable where the power is greatest. We must remember the context for this parable is given in the very first verse, "Then drew near unto him all the publicans and sinners for to hear him" (Luke 15:1). This parable was told to those who most needed it—and the hope it inspires. I would draw attention to the word *all* in that verse. This story is inclusive of every type of human failure and all personalities, with their various guilts and hesitations. He drew them all because none felt condemned in His presence. We know the story well. "I will arise and go to my father, and will say unto him, Father, I have sinned against heaven, and before thee, and am no more worthy to be called thy son: make me as one of thy hired servants. And he arose, and came to his father. But when he was yet a great way off, *his father saw him*, and had compassion, and ran, and fell on his neck, and kissed him" (Luke 15:18–20). To see those who desire to return while they are a great way off is a wondrous gift. Now when I read this most beloved parable, the Spirit bids me pray, "Father in Heaven grant me the eyes of Jesus that I may see those who are yet a great way off and run with compassion."

I wrote earlier of the woman taken in adultery, another of the great stories of Jesus so frequently told and loved. But I now read it looking for the Savior's vision and have found a beautiful phrase within the story that taught me something about the eyes of Jesus. "When Jesus had lifted up himself, *and saw none but the woman*" (John 8:10; emphasis added). I realize that, at face value, John is telling us the woman is now alone, since her accusers have been shamed by their own consciences into retreat, but I love the singular focus of the Savior on the woman. She was all that mattered at that moment—her needs, her emotions, her hope, her desire. Others saw her sin; Jesus saw "the woman." Though the multitude that Jesus had been teaching before the interruption were still there, they mattered not at all, nor, we may add, do the generations of onlookers who will read this story down through the ages. He is alone with her. He sees only her. There are in our encounters in life many who need to be seen as Jesus saw her, who need that type of individual understanding and concentrated attention. So now the Spirit invites me to pray: "Father in Heaven, grant me the eyes of Jesus that I may see 'none but the woman.'"

There was another woman who came to Jesus in her sorrow—Mary, the sister of Martha and Lazarus. When Jesus arrived after the burial of her brother, Mary came to Jesus outside of Bethany and fell at his feet, as had Martha earlier. "When *Jesus therefore saw her weeping . . . he groaned in the spirit, and was troubled*, and said, Where have ye laid him? They said unto him, Lord, come and see. *Jesus wept*" (John 11:33–35; emphasis added). I read these words and the Spirit encourages me to pray: "Father in Heaven, grant me the eyes of Jesus, that I too may groan in the Spirit when I see those who weep."

One last example before moving to the final stair: When Andrew first brought his brother Simon to see Jesus, the very first words he heard from the Savior's lips are instructive. John tells the story: "And he brought him to Jesus. When *Jesus beheld him, he said, Thou art Simon the son of Jona: thou shalt be called Cephas*, which is by interpretation, A stone" (John 1:42; emphasis added). The name *Peter* is the Latin word, *Cephas* the Greek. Jesus saw more than a fisherman, more than the son of Jona, more than Simon, he saw the untapped—unknown even to the man standing before him—strength and potential. Jesus saw *Cephas* in Simon. And the Spirit tells me to pray, "Father in Heaven, grant me the eyes of Jesus that I may see the Cephas in the Simons I meet." Surely all those we meet have Cephas within them. Our opportunity is to awaken this, especially in children and those closest to us. When the disciples were caught in the storm on the night Jesus walked on the water, we read: "*He saw them toiling in rowing*; for the wind was contrary unto them" (Mark 6:48). We too may pray, Father, give us the eyes of thy Son, that we may see those "toiling in rowing" when the winds of life are contrary to them. This is a beautiful stair, one that can be enhanced when we include in our search hearing with the ears of Jesus, touching with the hands of the Savior, and feeling with the heart of Christ.

THE STAIR OF CHARITY

Our climbing the stairs may come in a different order for everyone, but I believe the last and highest one on the great uplifting staircase is that of charity. This is such an obvious stair that I wrestle with what I can say. Just a few hours before I wrote this, I sat in a family home evening with my son's family in Kansas. My four-year-old granddaughter had been assigned the lesson and had been working on it all morning. She had no help or prompting from her mother, but busily cut something out of pink construction paper. She needed some tape and it was provided. When evening came and the attention was turned on her, she produced a line of pink hearts connected one to another with an abundance of scotch tape, one for each member of the family. She held up her string of pink hearts and said, "This is 'love one another.'" It was one of the best family home evening lessons I have ever heard. Five words and an object lesson! I can see her still in her footie pajamas, untamed hair falling everywhere, holding up her creation. I asked my daughter-in-law if she had coached this idea, but she assured me it was all Madalyn's. She was as surprised as the rest of us. I drew my granddaughter near and asked her again to tell me the lesson of the paper hearts. This time she said, "You can stick your heart next to mine." Four years old! That is the great lesson of mortality—learning how to stick your heart next to mine. Ultimately the chain, bound with an abundance of charity's tape, must include all human hearts.

Charity's grandeur pressed its awareness to me in a rather unexpected manner which I share with some hesitation. I fear that I will be misunderstood, but I can think of no greater way to lift it high enough up the stairway. There are multiple stories of the radiant beauty of sacrifice and unity we could explore, but I will try another way.

I have been very blessed in the latter years of my life to travel a great deal in many different nations. I have studied the culture, art, history, literature, and especially religion to prepare to teach about the countries we visit. I am impressed often by the dignity and beauty of the many truths and the goodness that the broad stretch of humankind has discovered and passed on. While seeking what to share with a group, I am always grateful when I find similarities to the great doctrinal foundations of the restored gospel, but I also experience wonder and depth when I find no connections. There are also parallels I've discovered in many places which leave me more and more amazed at the depth of Joseph Smith's mind. He had what I call "an old mind," so comfortable and aware of very ancient things. Having said this, I must confess a dilemma has also arisen. This has come mostly from a certain obsession I have developed for learning Chinese wisdom, but it is not limited to my searching here. I use it only as illustration.

What we call the plan of salvation or plan of happiness is the great doctrinal center of revealed and restored truth. At the core of this pillar of religious reality sits the Atonement of Christ. I anticipated finding echoes, shadows, hints, even simplifications of the plan of happiness and Atonement everywhere in the world, however obscured by man's additions and subtractions. Yet I have found no evidence that the Atonement or the plan of salvation with their many circling spokes united by this innermost pivotal hub was ever taught—or conceived—in Chinese thought. This also holds true for other philosophies in the world. LDS doctrine allows for teaching these principles in the spirit world, but the absence is a bit bewildering to me. China has enjoyed the longest single uninterrupted continuation of civilized history in the world. I couldn't begin to tell you what I've learned from them and how much I admire all things Chinese. They are a bright, intelligent people with moving and powerful literature, art, philosophy, and a tremendous amount of wisdom, but no impression of what we would consider the single most important truth seems to be found there. What do I do with this? I admit I may not have looked in all the right places, but if it is there and I simply haven't found it, it would be in a rather obscure setting and not in the mainstream of Chinese thinking.

If the Atonement cannot be found or is obscured in the wisdom and truths of China or other places in the world, there is one concept I *have* found in all places, and that distinctively prominent, whether the place be highly civilized or not. It is the need for love in all aspects of human relations. If knowledge or awareness of what we call the Atonement is missing in parts of the globe's history and geography, charity is not, though known by different names. For the Chinese, *benevolence* is the key word, emphasized and elevated to the highest level of human character. This was the essence of, for example, Confucius's thought, whose teaching was carried down through the various Chinese dynasties for roughly 2,500 years. In India, the key teaching arising from Siddhartha, later the Buddha, and enshrined in Buddhism is *compassion*. In Christianity, it is *charity*. These three words—charity, compassion, and benevolence—all portray the same thing and have been taught all over the world and in every age.

The scriptures affirm that there are two great commandments—to love God and to love our fellowmen (see Matthew 22:36–40). I find it interesting, perhaps significant, that one of the earliest times in the sacred record that these two are mentioned, the love of fellowmen is given the leading priority, or at least it is stated first. When speaking to Enoch about the wickedness of the people soon to be destroyed by the great flood, the Father said: "Unto thy brethren have I said, and also given commandment, that they should love one another, and that they should choose me, their Father" (Moses 7:33).

Jesus made the two great commandments His central teaching at the Last Supper. Since these were His final offerings just prior to his arrest and eventual crucifixion, their importance is enhanced. The Apostle John was so impressed with Christ's final thoughts that he made them the central emphasis in his gospel and also in his first epistle. Jesus stressed the need of love by example and word at the Last Supper. He simply taught that one shows her or his love of God by obedience, and her or his love of fellowmen by sacrifice and service. In this setting, He washed the disciples' feet, illustrating that there is no act of service too low, too apparently demeaning, that the highest of all of us would not need to do it. The great truth of leadership that few ever realize is that the leader exists to serve those who follow him; those who follow do not exist to serve the leader. Jesus understood this very well. "Ye call me Master and Lord: and ye say well; for so I am. If I then, your Lord and Master, have washed your feet; ye also ought to wash one another's feet" (John 13:13–14). In the words of my granddaughter, this is how we stick our hearts together.

Shortly thereafter, Jesus said, "A new commandment I give unto you, That ye love one another; as I have loved you, that ye also love one another" (John 13:34). I have pondered why Jesus called this a "new" commandment since it is as old as creation. True, but given the sad history of the world, it is a commandment that needs renewing each and every generation. The meaning of the word in Greek suggests this idea. *New* means "fresh" or "that which is unaccustomed or unused, not new in time, recent, but new as to form or quality, of different nature."[6] All followers of Jesus are under a divine command to love in an unaccustomed way, with fresh form or quality, different in nature from the way the world loves. It was the *living* of this commandment, not some demonstration of doctrinal purity or faith in certain beliefs about God that would determine who was or who was not a true disciple, a true Christian. "By this shall all men know that ye are my disciples, if ye have love one to another" (John 13:35). Let us also not forget that Paul, in what can arguably be called his greatest moment of teaching, placed charity even above faith. "And now abideth faith, hope, charity, these three; but the greatest of these is charity" (1 Corinthians 13:13).

When John thought later in his life about those last lovely moments the disciples shared with Jesus, he retaught the great commandments, stressing the truth that the love of others is the truest indication of one's love of God. "For this is the message that ye heard from the beginning, that we should love one another" (1 John 3:11). "Beloved, let us love one another: for love is of God; and every one that loveth is born of God, and knoweth God. He that loveth not knoweth not God; for God is love. . . . If God so loved us, we ought also to love one another. . . . He that loveth not his brother whom he hath seen, how can he love God whom he hath not seen? And this commandment have we from him, That he who loveth God love his brother also" (1 John 4:7–8, 11, 20–21).

One of my most beloved statements from the pen of the Prophet Joseph Smith was written while he was in Liberty Jail, the recipient of the religious, cultural, and political intolerances of his fellowmen. Still he could write: "There is a love from God that should be exercised toward those of our faith, who walk uprightly, which is peculiar to itself, but it is without prejudice; *it also gives scope to the mind, which enables us to conduct ourselves with greater liberality towards all that are not of our faith, than what they exercise towards one another.* These principles approximate nearer to the mind of God, because it is like God, or Godlike."[7] We might say these principles come *nearest* to the mind of God—the last stair upon which we all desire to stand. Mormon, when speaking of charity, indicated, "Charity is the pure love of Christ, and it endureth forever; and whoso is found possessed of it at the last day, it shall be well with him" (Moroni 7:47). Or, in the wisdom of a child, "You can stick your heart next to mine."

"I AM ROSE GISONDA"

I don't wish to belabor the many stairs. I have presented only a few by way of example either because they are obviously necessary, or because they are ones I wish devoutly to stand upon, or because there are those we might not be aware of. Before we move on up the stairway to the top, I would add a personal witness that along the way there is much encouragement and joy. The journey itself provides its own fulfillment, regardless of what awaits. This keeps us moving upward. May I relate only one example? I choose it because it is so recent in my life and yet connected to events many long years ago.

Nephi's brother Jacob presented to his people an intriguing idea that has demanded much reflection. Speaking of the judgment, he said, "The righteous shall have a perfect knowledge of their enjoyment, and their righteousness" (2 Nephi 9:14). This was also true of the opposites. What exactly is a "perfect knowledge?" I'm not sure, but it may have to do with a full realization of how our good acts have played out in the lives of others in a broader and deeper field. I served a mission in France in 1969–70. I must admit that France was one of the last places on earth I wished to go, largely due to my high school French teacher, who struck terror into my heart almost daily if I could not speak her language correctly. Her stare alone could drive every French word I had ever learned right out of my brain. I actually prayed fervently I would not go to France, but the call came and the letter said, "French

East Mission." Like many who served in Europe, I would have been happy just to see one person enter the Church. I knew this would be a challenging mission—and it was. However, my companions and I did see some success, especially in Grenoble during the first year of my mission. I explain this by way of background.

In 2013, I was with a tour group in Jerusalem. We always sing "I Am a Child of God" in St. Anne's Church because the acoustics are so remarkable. When we concluded, one of the couples told me a French woman wanted to speak to me. She and her husband were visiting the Holy Land on business, were members of the Church, and knew we were a Mormon group because of the song we had sung. My French is not so great after more than forty years, and she could speak no English, but in my own faltering way I was able to communicate with her. After a general conversation, she asked me where I learned to speak French. I told her I had served a mission in France. The next obvious question was "Where?" When I told her I had worked in Grenoble, she became excited and told me she had been baptized in Grenoble. So we talked about some of the members whom we both knew and the progress of the Church there since 1970. I had been talking with her close to an hour by this time. I asked her if she knew the Cortes family, and once again she brightened. She had served in a Relief Society presidency with Patricia Cortes, who was a young girl when I was in Grenoble. We had taught and baptized her and her parents. I cannot tell you how thrilled I was to hear all about the family and their activity including missions, temple marriages, and leadership.

We talked more while walking through the Old City and then she asked me if I knew the Gisonda family. "I certainly do," I answered, "I baptized the Gisonda family." "What is your last name?" she asked. I had not given it to her earlier, introducing myself simply as Mike. When I said, "Wilcox" she began to cry and embraced me tenderly. "I am Rose Gisonda," she said, "You're Elder Wilcox and you brought my family the gospel. You taught me when I was just a little girl. I was the youngest to be baptized with my parents and brothers and sisters."

The Gisonda family was Italian. Brother Gisonda's first wife had died and he had remarried. There were eight children from his first marriage and I learned that from the second marriage there were six additional children. They had all been raised in the Church, served missions, married in the temple, Rose told me. Then she said, "There are about one hundred and fifty people who are members of the Church because of what happened in Grenoble in 1969." I thought: *I'm living a Thomas S. Monson story! These things don't happen to ordinary members like me. I'm living a President Monson story! If he runs out of his own he can borrow mine!*

Since that day in Jerusalem, I have received several letters from both the Gisonda and the Cortes families, detailing their lives and contributions to the Church in France, including a kind and gracious letter from Sister Rachel Gisonda, presently serving a mission in London. And I hadn't wanted to go to France—I had prayed fervently that I would be sent somewhere else.

I remember our mission president telling us as soon as we arrived in France not to believe what he knew we had heard—that conversion came hard in France. "Believe what the Lord said, and what He tells you, 'The field is white already to harvest.'" I have a new understanding of the harvest now. It is not completed, not over and done, in our two years of service, but continues. I wonder how many missionaries who question what happened to those they taught or what they had accomplished will one day have a perfect knowledge of the good they have done in others' lives— beyond the lives they touched. These are the joys that come to us as we climb. We need not wait for the final glory at the top of the stairs.

CHAPTER SEVEN

THE CITY AT THE TOP OF THE STAIRS

I saw the transcendent beauty
Of the gate through which
The heirs of that kingdom will enter.

—D&C 137:2

"I Don't Remember That"

Over the years I have tried to understand the fullest and deeper meaning of the one word with which my experience with the crystal stairs ended: "Look." Before me stretched the great crystal city of light. I suppose that is what I was to look at, the home at the top of the stairs. However . . .

Single words in the scriptures, words like *come* or *remember*, can never cease to teach. "Look!" Celestial glory had to do with looking. What did He want me—what did He want us—to see? Our understanding of the top of the stairs is, in many ways, very limited. Descriptions of it are almost always couched in figurative language. But this was a world in which I had always been comfortable; in time the images came, leaving me to wonder and ponder as they always do and yet always calming and reassuring me. I suppose during the climbing I knew inherently that a judgment awaited us at the top of the stairs. *Judgment* is a word that has never instilled in me a feeling of peace or comfort. No, the judgment was something to feel anxious about. Would I pass the test? I so hated tests.

But I had the judgment all wrong. I believed it would focus mostly on my mistakes. If I missed heaven, it would be because of my failures, and I encountered them daily, weekly, continually. Sins—falling short of the mark—seemed to cling to me. And then they never seemed to leave me in peace. Once committed, they would haunt my memory. There were times I felt memory was not one of God's greatest gifts. Yet Ezekiel promised that all the "transgressions . . . shall not be mentioned [for those who were trying], so iniquity shall not be your ruin" (Ezekiel 18:22, 30). The Prophet Joseph Smith taught in the Doctrine and Covenants that "I, the Lord, remember them no more" (D&C 58:42). These promises were for the repentant, and those climbing the stairs were in a constant state of improvement. Repentance was not a single stair, but an attitude inherent in the climbing—part of the light streaming through them all. Those who continued climbing learned to love the very word, as did Alma in his beautiful hymn found in Alma 29. Maybe the judgment was about another aspect of our memory.

I have had moments of intense pondering concerning the judgment much like my inventory with the Lord at the seminary graduation in Tempe. During these reflections, the Spirit sometimes takes over my thinking and shows me scenes that teach. Perhaps I'm too concerned with the judgment. One such experience changed my whole perception of that time when, at the top of the stairs, our lives will be reviewed. It taught me one of the meanings of "Look!"

I was invited into the presence of the Savior, the eternal judge. The setting was nonthreatening, not a courtroom nor the Arizona interview, but a conversation room with two beautiful chairs set very close to each other. I was invited to sit down. Then the questions began, the first three being, "Did you preach the gospel? Did you redeem the dead? Did you perfect the Saints?" To be honest, I felt somewhat threatened with each question, but I answered as I am sure anyone would. I said, "Lord, I tried." To which he responded, "Let us see."

Then before my eyes, He presented scenes from my life, but to my great amazement, all He showed me were those experiences when I was successful in my attempts. I saw moments from my full-time mission and stake missions, times I spoke with friends, and prepared my children for their own missions. I saw my efforts to find my ancestors at the Family History library and every single temple session I had attended. All these were faithfully recorded. I saw every home teaching visit I had made in years of activity and all callings, as well as tiny moments and conversations with members, classes taught, firesides spoken at. I was surprised at the minuteness of detail being presented to me.

The questions continued, "Were you a good husband? Did you teach your children? Did you follow the Brethren? Did you improve on your talents and opportunities?" Each time I answered, "Lord, I tried." Each time the positive scenes appeared. But at the end of each series of scenes, my mind always filled with my failures.

"What about my failures?" I asked Him with each new question. "You did not show me my failures."

"Tell me your failures," He responded. Then I would pour out the many occasions I had *not* done missionary work as I should have, or did not go to the temple as I ought, or did not fulfill my callings as well as I wanted, or had neglected some important aspect of being a husband or father. My memory was replete with these things. It was always such a relief to tell Him. He listened quietly. Then, at the end of every one of my painful recitals of inadequacy, He said, "I don't remember that." Four simple words brushed away, as though it was all mere dust on the scales of mercy, my deepest regrets! I believe I now understand one of the beautiful meanings of "Look!" We are to look at the good we have done. All the rest, those nagging neglects and troubling mists of guilt, were not His focus and they should not be ours. Look upon the naked, unhidden beauty of your own lifetime of efforts to be good and obedient and true. None of the rest mattered. For Him, all was easy to forgive and to forget.

In Hans Christian Andersen's fairy tale *The Snow Queen*, Andersen begins the story with a magic mirror which distorts everything good, making it less and less attractive while emphasizing and enlarging the negative, until only the ugly and dark are reflected while the good and the noble diminish. The mirror is shattered into millions of pieces, which are blown all over the world. The glass dust gets into people's eyes and the distorted reflection of the original mirror continues to work. They begin to see themselves and others through the enchanted mirror's magic. Perhaps all of us have a little mirror dust in our eyes which causes us to view ourselves a bit too harshly, focusing on our failures and magnifying them while allowing our better moments to pale in comparison. We do this with others also. We must wash the mirror dust from our eyes.

When Laurie was struggling with the cancer in her brain, she had difficulty communicating, as the speech centers were being invaded. But during those months she seemed enshrouded in a calm, serene air, a breeze that I sensed was blowing from the world which she would soon enter. During one of those moments, when the fear of the spreading cancer was somewhat stilled, she said words which still bring tears, but not ones of sadness. "I feel no guilt. For the first time in my life I feel no guilt." She said it with a touch of surprise, a tiny tone of wonder. It was a washing, a cleansing time—all the inadequacies, failures, weaknesses, and lost opportunities for goodness were leaving. She would not take them into the mansions of her Father in Heaven. It was an end-of-life baptism, the grand atoning gift of Jesus, and I believe it waits at the top of the stairs for all who have climbed with diligence and a desire to please the Father as Jesus pleased His Father. What God looks at are the pluses not the minuses of our lives; they are what he wishes us so earnestly to see. "Look!"

Climbing the stairs seemed easier the higher one went. This means in part that, though we will always struggle to be better and better, we do conquer and endure and find it easier to lift ourselves above the distractions of the world. We are making progress in our Christlike search. We begin to see His image engraved in our own countenances. This creates hope and brings patience.

I think Laurie in those last months and weeks was looking at her own image as God held up His mirror and washed away the distorting mirror dust of Andersen's story. How very far she had come. Joseph Smith wrote: "We consider that God has created man with a mind capable of instruction, and a faculty which may be enlarged in proportion to the heed and diligence given to the light communicated from heaven to the intellect; and that the nearer man approaches perfection, the clearer are his views, and the greater his enjoyments, till he has overcome the evils of his life and lost every desire for sin; and like the ancients, arrives at that point of faith where he is wrapped in the power and glory of his Maker, and is caught up to dwell with Him. But we consider that this is a station to which no man ever arrived in a moment."[1]

The beauty of the climb is, however, that though it appears the stairs lift more gently as the climb rises, the truth is we are better able to handle the grade.

LOOK AT THE LIGHT

I am still learning the meaning of that single word, "Look!" and of the beautiful city. Learning about them almost always comes in the scenes of my imagination—sometimes in reflection, sometimes in dreams, sometimes in pondering on the scriptures, sometimes unexpectedly as a gift from heaven. I was twenty-three during my first year of teaching seminary and not much older than the seniors in my class. I admit I felt somewhat uncomfortable in the high school setting and was relieved when, after six years of teaching at that level, I was moved into a university setting. I had not enjoyed high school as a student and carried some of those unpleasant memories with me, yet had loved every aspect of college. I think some of the young men sensed my lack of confidence and took advantage of that. I felt challenged almost every day to hold onto control of the class. Two young men in particular were my nemeses. I used to hope that they would get sick and not show up on the days that I had prepared a lesson I wanted to go particularly well. Needless to say, and in all honesty, I did not like them. So the Lord took me in hand to teach me something about all human beings, but represented by these two young men.

One night while I was asleep, in a dream I found myself in prison with my two young students as companions. It is interesting the symbols the Spirit can form in the mind. I suppose I had considered myself in a prison of sorts with them. The prison was muddy; we were filthy; I was ashamed to see myself in such a state. We were walking in the exercise yard when a light from an unknown source began to lift us into the air and above the prison walls. It continued to lift us higher and higher. We could see the green countryside all around the muddied brown spot of the prison yard. As we rose into the air, the light grew in brightness. We watched the details of the landscape diminish. Then the edges of the continent appeared and finally the rounded horizons of the world itself. The earth grew smaller and smaller. As the world shrank into one tiny blink of light in a vast ocean of light we finally turned our attention away from it. In front of us stood a man clothed in white, radiant with light. He gave that same still, sweet command, "Look!" We looked at him, thinking that is what he meant, but he gently shook his head and smiled, repeating the single command, "Look!" Again we looked intently at him, but he smiled and pointed in our direction. "Look!" he said a third time. He was so anxious to show us something we had not yet discerned, but would give him great pleasure when we saw it. This time, however, we looked at each other. The light was flowing from us as radiantly as it was from him, from the two boys (the boys I did not like), from me.

How that mental image has changed my view of my fellowmen. At the top of the stairs we reach our full divine potential; that is a possibility for the least likely of souls. By this I do not mean that my two students were next-to-impossible candidates for celestial glory, but I perceived that the message was to learn to look at others, inasmuch as we can, with the eyes of God. He always sees the divinity in each individual. I was not seeing them the way He sees them. To view people this way, to see humanity this way, with all its problems, evils, and failings will enliven us and allow us in the worst of times to remain positive and optimistic about the human race. This was especially necessary for me as I began to teach the youth, for I would meet thousands of them over the years and I needed to know at the deepest level of consciousness exactly who and what they were and where they were going.

"WE SHALL BE LIKE HIM"

Perhaps John stated it best when, in his epistle to the early Saints, he told them about what awaited them in a future day if they would learn to love and live as Jesus did. He wanted them to know in what way God's great love was manifested towards them. "Behold, what manner of love the Father hath bestowed upon us," he began, "that we should be called the sons of God: therefore the world knoweth us not, because it knew him not. Beloved, now are we the sons of God, and it doth not yet appear what we shall be: but we know that, when he shall appear, we shall be like him; for we shall see him as he is" (1 John 3:1–2). The world does not understand, and frequently neither do we, the immensity of our own souls nor God's ultimate design in our creation. Isaiah's famous words, "Since the beginning of the world men have not heard, nor perceived by the ear, neither hath the eye seen, O God, beside thee, what he hath prepared for him that waiteth for him" (Isaiah 64:4), pertain not only to the immeasurable gift of His Son, but also the future destiny of all His sons and all His daughters if they will climb to the top of the stairs. If we can plant this idea in our hearts, not just in our minds, a distinct hope is born within, a necessary hope, for it will sustain us as we sort through our bags and packages and ascend the stairs. In John's epistle, he continues with the practical application of what he had written earlier, "And every man that hath this hope in him purifieth himself, even as he is pure" (1 John 3:3). Is not the climb one of continual purification—each step making us pure as the stair is pure? In the Book of Mormon, Moroni included a speech centered on charity and hope from his father, Mormon, because he felt that it was especially needed. Mormon concluded his oration with an appeal "with all the energy of heart" that we would pray for the love of Christ—that we would be filled with it. For if we were filled, "when he shall appear we shall be like him, for we shall see him as he is; that we may have this hope; that we may be purified even as he is pure" (Moroni 7:48). So the purity we seek is the purity of love. I have learned—I am still trying to learn—how much the climbing of the crystal stairs centers on an ability to love in ever-widening outward reaching. Is it not true that the higher we go, the more we see? This seeing, however, is the seeing of souls. When we do, we desire their happiness.

THE LIBRARY

Much later in my life, in a time of sadness, there was another time I was shown the Celestial City through my imagination. Instead of the Stair Builder waiting, a man and a woman walked through the open gate to greet me. They were my ancestors from some distant past. I did not know their names, but they knew me. As they walked forward, I could feel their love. They knew the sadness of my heart and had come to cleanse it. I thought as they moved toward me that I had never seen or felt such serenity before and sensed without words that celestial love finds its highest and perhaps its only happiness in the joy of others. At the bottom of the stairs and on the plain, everyone sought happiness in their own fulfillments. At the top, all effort was directed outward to the happiness of others. The giving of love is so much more important than the receiving. To be God or to be like God is to find your own most satisfying fulfillment in the joy of others—in the giving of love. At the top of the crystal stairs, the self was gone, with all self-directed desire, all ego, replaced with a longing to fulfill and bring about the happiness of their beloved.

"We want to show you something," my ancestors said, "that we believe will bring you great joy." I followed them into the city. The architecture of each building was so fitting that I knew its purpose by looking at it. We stopped in front of a building. "This is the library," they explained. We entered a large round room reaching many stories high, lined from top to bottom with many millions of beautifully bound volumes. I have loved books for as long as I can remember—their feel, their smell, the sound of turning pages, and the joy of reading. My favorite places in the many destinations which I have visited are libraries. There is a beautiful one in Vienna and several in the Potala Palace in Lhasa, Tibet. There is something so appealing to me about all the learning those leatherbound or boxed volumes contain. The room I think I most love in all the world is the library at Trinity College, Dublin. The architectural structure makes one feel like they are entering a giant book which stretches the whole length of the room, the ceiling arched like a binding. It is the closest place I have visited that equals in the tiniest way what the Spirit presented at this occasion.

My hosts were right. I was filled with happiness to see the lovely room which represented so much learning, so many gracious truths. They gave me time to take it all in, then said, "These are the scriptures from the numberless worlds created by our Father in Heaven." Of all the books written, do we not love the scriptures the most, for they contain some of the highest and most lovely truths of all? They describe the most perfect of beings. It made absolute sense to me that this knowledge would be preserved eternally, as all knowledge will be. The Apostle John wrote at the end of his gospel these wonderful words about his own desire to have written all the deeds of Christ—and he was referring to only this one world: "And there are also many other things which Jesus did, the which, if they should be written every one, I suppose that even the world itself could not contain the books that should be written. Amen" (John 21:25). That is such an appropriate way for the gospels to end—with a longing for greater knowledge. If the Savior visited and said, "You may ask me any question you like," I would ask Him to tell me more of the stories of His life.

During a difficult time in the early days of the Church, the Lord comforted His people with the promise of celestial light awaiting them in His eternal kingdom: "Yea, verily I say unto you, in that day when the Lord shall come, he shall reveal all things—things which have passed, and hidden things which no man knew, things of the earth, by which it was made, and the purpose and the end thereof—things most precious, things that are above, and things that are beneath, things that are in the earth, and upon the earth, and in heaven. And all they who . . . endure in faith, though they are called to lay down their lives for my sake yet shall they partake of all this glory" (D&C 101:32–35). *Glory* in this final sense suggests the glory of knowledge and learning. "The glory of God is intelligence, or, in other words, light and truth" (D&C 93:36). Do we not need to know "things of the earth, by which it was made" because we are to be creators ourselves? What glorious universities of thought will we be allowed to drink from! What questions our hungry minds will have to ask the Lord and what answers will He delight to grant us!

My two ancestral companions had one final thing to show me. "We have discussed among ourselves," they said, "which verse among all the volumes we will have you read." They reached for one of the bound books, opened it, and gave it to me. I read the words. They were powerful and beautiful, as the scriptures always are. I don't know how to describe the impact they had upon me. In the Book of Mormon, it was recorded of Jesus' prayer for the children, "No one can conceive of the joy which filled our souls at the time" (3 Nephi 17:17). Moroni once spoke of the words written by the Brother of Jared saying, "The things which he wrote were mighty even as thou art, unto the overpowering of man to read them" (Ether 12:24). That is how I felt. Though I was not allowed to remember past my dream the words themselves, I remember what they described. They spoke of the love of the Father for all His children, wherever they are found, and His desire that they be happy. I understood that the theme of all those thousands of books, the message of countless numbers of worlds, was one of love and joy. Learning rests at the top of the stairs. Love permeates all at the top of the stairs. Joy, of which our earthly joys are but an earnest replica, waits at the top of the stairs. Those blessings are no more powerfully portrayed than by John in both Revelation and in his choice of which of the Savior's appearances on Resurrection morning to include in his gospel.

When the Apostle John saw in vision "the holy city . . . prepared as a bride adorned for her husband" (Revelation 21:2), he described what God will do for those who enter therein. "And God shall wipe away all tears from their eyes; and there shall be no more death, neither sorrow, nor crying, neither shall there be any more pain: for the former things are passed away." These words were followed by an urgent command by the Lord that this particular promise be written down so all could read it forever. "And he said unto me, Write: for these words are true and faithful." When it was done, Jesus said, "I am Alpha and Omega, the beginning and the end" (Revelation 21:4–6). Perhaps these words best convey what waits at the end of the climb. We ponder: "What is He the beginning and the end of?" People sometimes ask me if I have a favorite spot in the Holy Land. That is always a difficult question to answer, for there are many places that speak to my heart, but there is one scripture story that I always look forward with the greatest anticipation to read and share, and one place to do it. The story is Jesus' visit to Mary Magdalene at the Garden Tomb on Easter morning. I think in that one poignant moment of mercy we catch the essence of Christ, the meaning of John's vision of the Celestial City, and the fulfilled hope that waits at the top of the stairs.

THE MARY-AND-MASTER MOMENTS

In John's account of Resurrection morning, Mary Magdalene came alone to the tomb, "early, when it was yet dark" (John 20:1). When she arrived, the tomb was empty. We must do our best with our imagination and the Spirit's help to put ourselves in Mary's position. In doing so, we invite additional insight. Not many hours earlier she had stood at the foot of the cross and watched the Savior she loved die slowly, in great pain. She does not yet understand the true purpose of His mission. None of those great personalities of early Christianity did. She is confused, despairing, filled with sorrow, mourning, tearful, thinking of all the highest hopes and joyful expectations she had only a few hours ago that are now lost. He is dead and even His body is gone. She runs to tell Peter and John. The possibility of His resurrection is not present in her mind. "They have taken away the Lord out of the sepulchre, and we know not where they have laid him" (John 20:2). Her use of the plural *we* suggests she was accompanied, as in the synoptic gospel accounts, by other women, but John focuses solely on her. Peter and John run to the empty tomb, enter, see the grave clothes, then leave. Mary follows them out of the tomb, but remains—alone now—in the garden. We are specifically told that "as yet they knew not the scripture, that he must rise again from the dead" (John 20:9). He is gone; the sight of the empty tomb is the final reminder of all she has lost.

She has reached the bottom of despair. Her last act of devotion has been denied her.

"Mary stood without at the sepulchre weeping: and as she wept, she stooped down, and looked into the sepulchre" (John 20:11). This is such a human thing to do. She knows he is not there, but she looks again. Perhaps she sees the light of the angels now in the tomb, or a movement. As she looks, she sees the angels, who ask her, "Woman, why weepest thou?" In her grief, does she make the connection that these are angels? Perhaps they aren't radiant with glory, just dressed in white, but she's been at the tomb all this time and must know they are messengers from heaven, yet she opens her heart's sorrow as if they were human. There is no need for them to say, "Fear not." What is she thinking when they ask her the question? There is only one thing in her focus. "They have taken away my Lord, and I know not where they have laid him" (John 20:13). That is her only concern. She has not only lost Him in life, she has lost Him now in death. I have tried to put myself in Mary's position, which is a good and proper thing to do with all scripture stories, though with some reserve and caution. We all know grief and loss to some degree, and since the passing of my wife, it is easier for me to make Mary's heart my own. I am not sure what Mary was thinking, but at this moment in her life she seems to me to represent and embody in one human heart all the fallen hopes, the pain, the suffering, the sorrow, the loss, the disappointment, the despair of humanity. Her soul is your soul and my soul! Neither human nor angelic voice can move her from her lament: "They have taken away my Lord."

"And when she had thus said, she turned herself back, and saw Jesus standing, and knew not that it was Jesus" (John 20:14). I have wondered why she turned back. Did she feel someone was behind her? Was there nothing more to say to the angels? If the gardener can help her, then to him she will speak. I sense something deeper than her sorrow in this turning back, indicative of her desolation. She is so close to the end of pain but does not yet know it. Then Jesus addresses her. I have never been able to read the Savior's words to Mary with enough tenderness. I try to always read the scriptures aloud, but I just can't get to the depth of compassion implicit in His words. "Woman, why weepest thou? whom seekest thou?" (John 20:15). Believing him to be the gardener, she renews her lament—the singular focus of her thought. I must find him!

"Sir," she says, "if thou have borne him hence, tell me where thou hast laid him, and I will take him away" (John 20:15). I've never been able to read those words with the poignancy they awake in me, either. Then we are invited into one of the most beautiful scenes of lifting, of dramatic awakening, of profound change, of movement from opposites, of the grand purpose of God, of the top of the stairs perhaps in all scripture, in all literature. We understand in two simple words, one from each person—two names—exactly what it means for Jesus to say, "I am the beginning and the end."

"Jesus saith unto her, Mary. *She turned herself*, and saith unto him . . . Master" (John 20:16; emphasis added). That is all we need. John wrote it beautifully. Any more would be too much. I also love the three words, "She turned herself." Can we begin to understand the dramatic emotional shift in Mary at that moment? In one brief second, all the pain, sorrow, grief, confusion, loss, desperation is swept away and replaced with joy, gladness, amazement, love, life fulfillment. "I am the end of sorrow and tears!" Jesus is saying in that one word, that one name. "I am the beginning of peace and eternal happiness." He has taken her from the pain of the cross to the life-everlasting serenity of the Resurrection. She turned herself from the empty tomb to the living Christ. We too will turn from empty tombs of our own lives, whatever those tombs represent, to hear our names spoken in love by our Savior.

I don't know how to describe in words what those verses do to me every time I read them. It seems that all Christ came to earth for is encompassed in those two names, in that turning.

"Mary . . ."

"Master . . ."

We hold so close, in our cupped hands, all God desires for us and has prepared for us: the change, the amending, the movement, the healing, the divine transformation, the final turning, the divine night-to-day rotation from one opposite to the other. "It must needs be, that there is an opposition in all things" (2 Nephi 2:11), Lehi testified, but we know which of the opposites God has prepared for his children. (We see the same dramatic turning in Alma's account of God lifting him from the pains of hell to the peace of His presence in Alma 36.) And He can do it with a single word, the mere calling of our name. The tears are wiped away, but more, they are replaced by tears of a deeper emotion—that of love, of peace beyond thought, and fulfillment past expectation. Sorrow, pain, and grief were buried in the tomb; there would be no stone rolled away to allow them to live again. At that moment, what more could Mary ask? Life is fulfilled. She's at the top of the stairs entering the Eternal City; only the lessons and character-shaping marks of mortality's sorrows are left to create the eternal soul. Pain is removed, its hollow filled now with "joy unspeakable and full of glory" (1 Peter 1:8). As Eve stated so perfectly, "It is better for us to pass through sorrow . . ." The passage is finished ". . . that we may know." Now we *do* know. Part of our joy is the assurance that God Himself could not have told us in quite the same way that the passage, the climb, was worth all it demanded of us. Like the Hindu parable of Vishnu teaches, there are some things that can't be explained—they must be experienced.

I believe that the "Mary-and-Master" moment, the God-turning, awaits us all. Not that we don't have them in smaller portions now, but the grand one bids us forward against all arresting forces. We climb for that culmination. We'll know the time when all our pains, disappointed dreams, sorrows, inadequacies, guilt, and life-lacking fulfillments will move aside with the simple calling of our names. None of it will matter. Our burdens will leave us with greater compassion, kindness, mercy, gentleness, and patience, for that is what the cross-moments of our lives create, but we will not be ever-learning the tutorials of empathy. They will come to fruition. Jesus asks us, in that same voice of tenderness I try to capture whenever I read the story, "Why weepest thou?"—knowing that our tears will all have an end soon, as He knew Mary's would. (As He also knew Mary and Martha's would when His compassion-heart wept with them at Lazarus's tomb.) The day will come when I will hear my own name called and, turning, will see not only my Savior, but my Laurie as well.

"Michael . . ."

"Master . . ."

Then loss and grief will truly be over and happiness as only God comprehends it can begin.

LOVE'S PUREST JOYS RESTORED

Sometime prior to the discovery of the cancer in Laurie that would take her life, I was preparing a lesson on the celestial kingdom, pondering as only reading the scriptures can motivate, when I sensed that gentle, teaching Spirit close to me. Sometimes it comes so quietly you don't know how long it has been there; you only notice that it has come. When I became aware of it,

I was asked a question: "Do you want to see the celestial kingdom?" I did not know how to answer, but thought, *If it would please you to show it to me.*

"It would be pleasing," came back the impression. I thought I would see unbelievably beautiful scenery, or mansions that would dwarf the highest aspirations of man. Yet none of this came into my mind. Instead, I was shown a woman. She was young, and warm, and love flowed out from her toward me. She was smiling, radiant, and dressed in white. Her eyes were bright green and her white hair flowed in long waves down her back. God showed me my wife. Here was a truth to be wondered at! Of all the glories one could know of God's eternal house, it was a relationship He chose to reveal, one cherished aspect of human love striving to become godly love! I suppose celestial glory is not so much a place or an environment as it is love between people, with all the fears, insecurities, failures, inadequacies, misunderstandings, doubts, and uncertainties removed, the sealing altars of the temple stronger than death, stronger even than our own human weakness. We sing from time to time:

> *Be still, my soul: the hour is hastening on*
> *When we shall be forever with the Lord,*
> *When disappointment, grief, and fear are gone,*
> *Sorrow forgot, love's purest joys restored.*
> *Be still, my soul: When change and tears are past,*
> *All safe and blessed we shall meet at last.*[2]

That too, and for me in particular, is worth the climb.

Epilogue

"Pass and Continue Beyond"

Whoso cometh in at the gate
And climbeth up by me
Shall never fall;
Wherefore blessed are they . . .
For they shall come forth
With songs of everlasting joy.

—Moses 7:53

The View from the Top

The living, climbing, and reaching can be invigorating. Not just the destination holds happiness and reward, but the journey itself. It took me years to learn this, so focused was I on the outcome. I recall one summer hiking in Glacier National Park. Early in the morning, my brother-in-law and I decided to climb to the top of a pass overlooking a beautiful glacial lake. It took us all morning to reach the timberline, but I remember the feeling of suddenly rising above the trees and seeing the vistas around us. The lake was far below and peaks of glacier-covered granite, interspersed with descending waterfalls, rose high above us. We

135

reached the pass, a long, low saddle of land stretching between two mountain ranges, just before noon but it no longer satisfied our desire to climb. We now wanted the peaks. We chose the highest one and climbed up. It was exhausting; the air thinned and our muscles ached, but the views grew more spectacular with each thousand feet in elevation we climbed. I reached a moment on that climb when I was really hurting, but I said to myself, "I am going to stand on that peak and nothing will stop me." And we did! Standing at the top of the world is a joy like no other. We descended to our camp wrapped in that glow of happiness that comes when you have given all you have and then one step more. Then the Spirit took that experience and taught me truth in just five words: "In like manner, master life." Here was the invitation yet again to climb the crystal stairs and achieve a higher summit.

When we reach the celestial city of light, will there be new stairways to climb? This thought has occupied my thinking from time to time. We believe in eternal progression; is the view from the top one that looks downward or upward still? I will not enter into new speculations about the eternal eons that wait, but will simply close with a few verses from Walt Whitman's *Song of Myself* that might serve as a prelude to the eternities that stretch beyond the crystal stairs:

> *This day before dawn I ascended a hill and look'd at the crowded heaven,*
> *And I said to my spirit When we become the enfolders of those orbs, and the pleasure*
> *And knowledge of every thing in them, shall we be fill'd and satisfied then?*
> *And my spirit said No, we but level that lift to pass and continue beyond.*[1]

NOTES

INTRODUCTION: THE POWER OF PARABLE

1. Joseph Smith, in *History of The Church of Jesus Christ of Latter-day Saints*, 7 vols., edited by B. H. Roberts (Salt Lake City: The Church of Jesus Christ of Latter-day Saints, 1932–51), 1:299.

CHAPTER ONE: THE WASTELAND AND THE WANDERERS

1. Matthew Arnold, "Dover Beach," in *The Works of Matthew Arnold* (Ware, Hartfordshire, UK: Wordsworth Editions, 1995), 402.
2. T. S. Eliot, "The Waste Land," lines 403–5, in *The Waste Land: Authoritative Text, Contexts, Criticism*, Michael North, ed. (New York: W.W. Norton, 2001), 18–19.
3. Philip Paul Bliss, "More Holiness Give Me," *Hymns of The Church of Jesus Christ of Latter-day Saints* (Salt Lake City: The Church of Jesus Christ of Latter-day Saints, 1985), no. 131.
4. William Wordsworth, "Ode: Intimations of Immortality from Recollections of Early Childhood," lines 59–66, 162–68, in *The Complete Poetical Works of William Wordsworth*, ed. Alice George (Boston: Houghton Mifflin, 1932), 354, 355.

CHAPTER TWO: THE STAIRWAYS OF MEN

1. George Lucas, Lawrence Kasdan, and Leigh Brackett, *Star Wars, Episode V: The Empire Strikes Back* (Los Angeles: 20th Century Fox, 1980).

CHAPTER THREE: THE CRYSTAL STAIRS
AND THE STAIR BUILDER

1. Joseph Smith, *Joseph Smith* (manual), in Teachings of Presidents of the Church series (Salt Lake City: The Church of Jesus Christ of Latter-day Saints, 2007), 268.
2. Fyodor Dostoyevsky, as quoted in Daniel J. Boorstin, *The Creators* (New York: Vintage Books, 1992), 662–63.
3. William Shakespeare, *Macbeth*, in *William Shakespeare: The Complete Works, Second Edition*, ed. Stanley Wells and Gary Taylor (Oxford: Clarendon Press, 2005), 5.5.23–27.

CHAPTER FOUR: SHATTERING THE STAIRS

1. C. S. Lewis, *The Problem of Pain* (New York: HarperCollins, 2001), 126.
2. Lewis Carroll, *Alice's Adventures in Wonderland* and *Through the Looking Glass and What Alice Found There* (New York: Penguin, 1998), 56.
3. Henry F. Lyte, "Abide with Me!" *Hymns of The Church of Jesus Christ of Latter-day Saints* (Salt Lake City: The Church of Jesus Christ of Latter-day Saints, 1985), no. 166.

CHAPTER FIVE: CLIMBING THE CRYSTAL STAIRS

1. See also Dieter F. Uchtdorf, "The Merciful Obtain Mercy," *Ensign*, May 2012, 70, 75–77.
2. Hyrum L. and Helen Mae Andrus, *They Knew the Prophet* (Salt Lake City: Bookcraft, 1974), 144.
3. William Shakespeare, *Measure for Measure*, in *William Shakespeare: The Complete Works, Second Edition*, ed. Stanley Wells and Gary Taylor (Oxford: Clarendon Press, 2005), 2.2.66–68.
4. William Shakespeare, *Measure for Measure*, in *William Shakespeare:*

The Complete Works, Second Edition, ed. Stanley Wells and Gary Taylor (Oxford: Clarendon Press, 2005), 2.2.75–81.

5. Mou Tzu, quoted in P. T. Welty, *The Asians: Their Heritage and Their Destiny* (New York: HarperCollins, 1953, 1976), reprinted in Kevin Reilly, *Readings in World Civilizations*, vol. 1, 2d. ed. (New York: St. Martin's Press, 1994), 165–70.

6. Claire Tomalin, *Charles Dickens: A Life* (New York: Penguin, 2011), 210.

7. Thomas S. Monson, "The Service That Counts," *Ensign*, November 1989, 46.

8. Jenny Hartley, *Charles Dickens and the House of Fallen Women* (London: Methuen, 2008), 93.

9. *Life and Letters of Charles Darwin*, ed. Francis Darwin, 2 vols. (New York: D. Appleton and Co., 1887), 1:81–82.

10. John Lennon and Paul McCartney, "Let It Be," *Let It Be* (London: Apple Records, 1970).

CHAPTER SIX: THE ASCENT CONTINUES

1. John Chrysostom, "The Easter Sermon of John Chrysostom," available at http://stpeterparish.com/documents/Faith%20Fact %20Easter%20Sermon.pdf; accessed 12 September 2014.

2. Emma Lou Thayne, "Where Can I Turn for Peace?" *Hymns*, no. 129.

3. Benjamin Franklin, *Autobiography of Benjamin Franklin* (Philadelphia: J. B. Lippincott & Co., 1869), 223.

4. Benjamin Franklin, *Memoirs of Benjamin Franklin*, 2 vols. (New York: Derby & Jackson, 1859), 1:37.

5. Galileo, in Stillman Drake, *Essays on Galileo and the History and Philosophy of Science, Volume 1* (Toronto: University of Toronto Press, 1999), 59.

6. W. E. Vine, *Vine's Expository Dictionary of New Testament Words* (New Jersey: Barbour and Company, 1940), 109.

7. Joseph Smith, in *History of The Church of Jesus Christ of Latter-day Saints*, 7 vols., edited by B. H. Roberts (Salt Lake City: The Church of Jesus Christ of Latter-day Saints, 1932–51), 3:304; emphasis added.

CHAPTER SEVEN: THE CITY AT THE TOP OF THE STAIRS

1. Joseph Smith, *Joseph Smith* (manual), in Teachings of Presidents of the Church series (Salt Lake City: The Church of Jesus Christ of Latter-day Saints, 2007), 210–11.
2. Katharina von Schlegel, translated by Jane Borthwick, "Be Still, My Soul," *Hymns*, no. 124.

EPILOGUE: "PASS AND CONTINUE BEYOND"

1. Walt Whitman, "Song of Myself," 46, lines 20–23; in *Major Writers of America*, Perry Miller, ed. (New York: Harcourt, Brace & World, 1966), 600.

INDEX

Abraham, 16, 17, 35–36, 48–49

Acceptance, of circumstances, 89

Action, salvation through, 59–60

Adultery, woman taken in, 74, 107

Agency, 24, 31–32

Alice in Wonderland (Carroll), 54–55

Ambition, 45, 87

Ancestors, vision of author's, 125–28

Andersen, Hans Christian, 120

Andrew, 108

Arnold, Matthew, 9

Atonement: understanding of, 61; at core of plan of salvation, 110–11

Babel, Tower of, 21–24

Bags, in parable of crystal stairs, 4–5

Beauty, in world and mortality, 7–8, 12

Becoming, 59–64

Being, 59–64

Benevolence, 111

Bread of life discourse, 50

Buddhism, 111

Burning bush, 79–82

Celestial City, vision of, 34–35, 117–18, 125–28. *See also* Heaven, righteousness as way to

Celestial kingdom, author's vision of, 133–34

Change, 89

Charity: and following Jesus Christ's example, 54, 124–25; faith and, 62–63; in writings of Paul, 66; unity and, 69–70;

gossip and, 75; humility and, 103; stair of, 109–14

Charles (Church investigator), fears answer to prayer, 51–52

Children: learning from, 21–22; teaching, 33

Children of God, divine identity of, 19–20

Chinese wisdom, 110–11

Choices, reaching consensus in group, 69–70. *See also* Agency

Chrysostom, John, 96, 97–98

Church of Jesus Christ of Latter-day Saints, The: teachings of men versus, 27–30; reconciling mortal realities with teachings of, 39–43; questions regarding culture of, 68–71

Circumstances, contentment in, 88–89

Coin in fish's mouth, 90–91

Commandments: obedience to, 93–94; to love God and one another, 111–13

Comparing ourselves with others, 74–75

Compass, internal, 32–33

Compassion, 97, 107, 111

Compromise, in areas of integrity, 48–49

Confrontation, avoiding, 92

Confucius, 38, 111

Conscience, 69

Contentment, 87–90

Corinthians, 27, 65–66

Criticism, 92

Crosby, Jesse, 72

Crystal stairs, parable of, 1–6

Cultural pursuits, 82–86

Cultural questions, 68–71

Darwin, Charles, 85

Despising others, 66–71

Determinism, 31

Dickens, Charles, 81–82, 84

Difficult students, 122–23

Divine identity, of God's children, 19–20

Dostoyevsky, Fyodor, 42

Dream: about straying students, 10–13; of Jacob, 25; of being saved by Jesus Christ, 98–99; of difficult students in prison, 122–23

Dress and grooming, 67–68

Earth, in vision of Celestial City, 35

Easter Sermon, 96, 97–98

Education, 82–86

Eliot, T. S., 9

Entertainment, 83–86

Erasmus of Rotterdam, 78

Eternal progression, 136

Exaltation, 37–38, 39

Eyes of Jesus, seeing others through, 105–8, 123

Failure(s), 44–45, 119–21

Fairness, mercy and, 96–97

Faith: in Jesus Christ, 61; transformation of definition of, 62–63

Family home evening lesson, 109

Fasting, 68

Fault finding, 71

Fish(es): coin in mouth of, 90–91; miracle of multitude of, 93

Foils, 25

Forgiveness, 60–61, 73

Franklin, Benjamin, 100–101

Galileo, 102

Gambling, 67

Garden Tomb, 128–32

Gate of heaven, 25–27

Gentile converts, 66, 69

Gisonda, Rose, 115–16

Giving up, 62

Glacier National Park, 10–11, 135–36

Gladness, finding, 18–19. See also Happiness; Joy

Glory, 127

God: love for, 13; unity with, 20; trying to live independently of, 24–25; reunion with, 26; reconciling mortal realities with loving, 39–43; becoming like, 60; and easing suffering, 80–82; mercy of, 96–98; commandment to love, 111–12

Godliness, linking contentment to, 88

Goodness: in world and mortality, 7–8, 12; attracts goodness, 32–33; relationship between light and, 35; focusing on, 119–21

Grace: acquired by Jesus Christ, 36–38; forgiving and enabling, 63

Greek Orthodox churches, 96

Grief, end of, 132–33

Grooming, 67–68

Guilt, 119–21

Habits, replacing, 14–15

Hall, Newton, 82

Happiness: fullness of, 54; in joy of others, 125; sorrow, pain, and grief replaced by, 132–33; in journey, 135–36. See also Gladness, finding; Joy

Hard sayings, 49–53

Heaven, righteousness as way to, 21–22. See also Celestial City, vision of; Celestial kingdom, author's vision of

Hindu parable, 55–58

Home, longing for, 16–20

Humility, 100–105

Idleness, 86

Idols, meat offered to, 65–66

Inclusion, 76–79

Integrity, 48–49

Intelligence: need for, 24; attracts intelligence, 33

Internal compass, 32–33

Jacob, dream of, 25

James, 45

Jesus Christ: love for, 13–15, 61; seeking, 15–16; reunion with, 26; teachings of men versus,

27–30; progression of, 36–38; following example of, 37, 38, 41–42, 54, 124–25; love of, 46; hard sayings of, 50–51; commitment to, 51; as only way, 53; becoming like, 60–64; faith in, 61; and woman taken in adultery, 74; contentment of, 87; chooses not to give offense, 90–94; mercy of, 96–100; seeing others through eyes of, 105–8, 123; issues commandment to love God and one another, 111–13; judgment of, 119–20; Resurrection of, 128–32. *See also* Atonement

Jews, contention between Gentile converts and, 66, 69

John the Baptist, 36–37

John the Beloved: vision of, 34–35; rebuke of, 45; and commandment to love one another, 112, 113

Journey, happiness in, 135–36

Joy: finding, 18–19; as purpose of life, 30–31; happiness in, of others, 125. *See also* Happiness

Judging others, 66–73

Judgment, 61–62, 114, 118–20

Justice, mercy and, 96–97

Knowledge: Abraham's desire for, 35–36; longing for greater, 126–27

Krishnamurti, Jiddu, 89

Labor, 87

Laborers in the vineyard, parable of, 96

Ladder, Jacob's dream of, 25

Lake Elizabeth, 10–11

Last Supper, 112

Leadership, persuasion as first principle of righteous, 64–66

Learned men, 102

Learning, 82–86

Leaves, oak, 14

Lehi, 29–32

Lewis, C. S., 44–45

Library, vision of celestial, 126–28

Life. *See* Mortality

Light: attracts light, 32–33, 36; relationship between truth and, 35

Literature, 84–85

Love: for Jesus Christ and Heavenly Father, 13–15; in spite of harsh mortal realities, 41–42; for mankind, 45–46; of Jesus Christ, 46; need for, as universal concept, 111; commandments regarding, 111–13; and following Jesus Christ's example, 124–25; giving, 125

"Love one another" object lesson, 109

Mary Magdalene, 128–32

Mary of Bethany, 107–8

Maya, 55–57

Measure for Measure (Shakespeare), 73

Meat, offered to idols, 65–66

Memory: of sins, 118; of weaknesses and failures, 119–21

Men, teachings of, 27–30, 32, 55

Mercy, 73, 96–100

Messiah, expectations for, 50

Middle East, 78–79

Millett, Joseph, 82

Mission, of author, 114–16

Moral life, destruction of, 9–13

Mortality: depicted as wasteland, 1–6, 8–10; beauty and goodness in, 7–8, 12; as valley of shadow of death, 15; strangers and wanderers in, 16–20; finding joy in, 18–19; premortal existence, 30; reconciling gospel truths with harsh realities of, 39–43; contentment in, 88–89. *See also* World

Moses, 80

Motes and beams, 70–73

Mou Tzu, 78

Myanmar, author buys postcard in, 88

Naaman, 22–23

Narada, parable of, 55–58

Nationality, 76–77

"Nevertheless," 90–94

"Notwithstanding," 90–94

Oak tree, 14

Obedience: follows love, 13–14; struggling with, 46–47; to commandments, 93–94; showing love through, 112

"Ode—Intimations of Immortality from Recollections of Early Childhood" (Wordsworth), 17–18

Offense: getting over past, 47; avoiding, 90–94

Oneness, 26, 66, 70

Opposition, 132

Orthodoxy, 96

Overconfidence, 24–25

Pain, end of, 132–33

Parable(s): of crystal stairs, 1–6; Hindu, 55–58; of laborers in the vineyard, 96; of prodigal son, 106–7

Patriotism, 76–77

Paul, 27–29, 65–66, 69, 87–88

Perfection: relationship between truth and, 35, 60; chances for, 44–45; Joseph Smith on achieving, 121

Persuasion, 64–66

Peter, 45, 51, 63, 90–91, 93, 108

PhD, author's experience getting, 61, 101–2

Pilgrims, mortals as, 16–20

Plan of happiness, 22–23, 110–11

Postcard, homemade, 88

Prayer, investigator fears answer to, 51–52

Premortal existence, 19–20

Pride, 45, 74–75, 100–105

Prison, author's dream of students in, 122–23

Prodigal son, 106–7

Progression, 36–38, 136
Purity, 20, 124–25

Qualities, Christlike: development of, 59–62; persuasion, 64–66; judging others, 66–73; not taking interest in others' weaknesses, 74–76; inclusion and tolerance, 76–79; easing suffering, 79–82; refinement, 82–86; contentment, 87–90; not giving offense, 90–94

Reason, need for, 24
Refinement, 82–86
Relativism, 31
Religion: truth in, 53–54; and quality of soul, 60
Repentance, 118
Resurrection, 128–32
Righteousness: as way to heaven, 21–22, 53; as happiness, 30–31; knowledge and, 36

Sabbath, 68
Sarah, 16, 17
Satan, 8, 11–12
Scriptures: purpose of, 15; children's understanding of, 21–22; vision of, 126
Sealing, 26
Sea of Galilee, 98–99
Sea of glass, 34–35
Selfishness, 48
Service, 40–41, 79–82, 112
Sin: parting with, 44–48; taking

interest in others,' 74–76; memory of, 118
Smith, Joseph, 34–35, 71–73, 110, 113, 121
Snow Queen, The (Andersen), 120
Sodom, 48–49
Song of Myself (Whitman), 136
Song of the Lord, 18–19
Sorrow, end of, 132–33
Soul, qualities of, 59–60. See also Qualities, Christlike
Spiritual progression, 36–38
Staircases: in parable of crystal stairs, 2–3; of men, 22; Jacob's dream of, 25
Strangers, mortals as, 16–20
Students: dream about straying, 10–13; dream about difficult, 122–23
Suffering, 39–43, 80–82

Taste, refining, 84–85
Teaching career, of author, 103–5, 122
Telestial glory, 39
Temple, 25–26, 27
Temple recommends, 46–47
Thread, compared to compromising integrity, 48–49
Time, use of, 82–86
Tithing, 47
Tolerance, 76–79
Tomalin, Claire, 82
Tower of Babel, 21–24
Tribute money, 91
Truth: in non-LDS beliefs, 22, 53–54, 78; versus teachings of men,

28–29, 32; relationship between light and, 35; internalization of, 35–36; reconciling mortal realities with gospel, 39–43; response to, 60

Unity, 26, 66, 70
Urania Cottage, 81
Urim and Thummim, 35

Valley of the shadow of death, 15
Virtue, 33
Vishnu, parable of, 55–58

Wasteland, mortality depicted as, 1–6, 8–10
Weaknesses: replacing, 14–15; parting with, 44–48; judging others for, 66–73; taking interest in others,' 74–76; memory of, 119–21

Whitman, Walt, 136
Wilcox, Laurie, 26–27, 76–77, 120–21, 133–34
Wilcox, Madalyn, 109
Wisdom, 33
Woman taken in adultery, 74, 107
Word of Wisdom, 67
Wordsworth, William, 17–18
Work, 87
World: beauty and goodness in, 7–8, 12; coming out of, 12–13; as valley of shadow of death, 15; strangers and wanderers in, 16–20; in thinking and decision making, 55. *See also* Mortality
Worship, 36–38

Zacchaeus, 106
Ziggurat, Tower of Babel as, 23